Gorilla Dawn

Eric Campbell

MACMILLAN CHILDREN'S BOOKS

First published 2001 by Macmillan Children's Books

This edition published 2001 by Macmillan Children's Books
a division of Macmillan Publishers Limited
25 Eccleston Place, London SW1W 9NF
Basingstoke and Oxford
www.macmillan.com

Associated companies throughout the world

ISBN 0 330 37167 3

1 3 5 7 9 8 6 4 2

A CIP catalogue record for this book is available from the British Library.

Phototypeset by Intype London Ltd
Printed and bound in Great Britain by Mackays of Chatham plc, Kent

For my granddaughter, Erica Ann

Follow thy fair sun, unhappy shadow.
                    Thomas Campion 1567–1620

Extract from *The Times*, London, 20 June 1966

Cambridge Anthropologist Missing

The anthropologist, Doctor Jane Hudson (26), daughter of the award-winning zoologist, Professor David Hudson of Cambridge University, has been reported missing in remote mountain terrain in Rwanda, Central Africa. Doctor Hudson, who was making a study of the behaviour of the rare Mountain Gorilla (*gorilla gorilla beringei*) in the Virungas, failed to return to her base camp two weeks ago. A search has been instituted by the Rwandan authorities. The area is reported to be inhospitable and frequented by poachers, smugglers and rebel forces opposed to the Rwandan Government. Fears are growing for Doctor Hudson's safety.

One

Kigali, Rwanda, Central Africa
Present Day

'Don't be downhearted, Anna.'

'I can't help it.'

'We'll be back soon. When this tragedy clears itself up.'

'Yes, I know,' Anna said.

But she knew in her heart that her father, with the best of intentions, was lying. They wouldn't be back soon. Perhaps they would never be back.

Alfred seemed to know that too. He rolled his eyes upwards and stared at Anna without lifting his head. Anna crossed the room, lay down beside the huge ridgeback and put her arm across his shoulder. The dog growled softly in appreciation and lifted one ear.

'It's all right, Alfred. Joseph will look after you when we're gone.'

The dog frowned at her.

'*He will*. Don't look at me like that.'

Another lie. How could they expect Joseph to stay and look after the house when everybody else was fleeing? Alfred would be left to fend for himself. To survive if he could.

Anna turned her face away. Guilty.

1

Alfred snorted and let his head fall back on to his smelly rug.

'Yes, that's it. Have the last word, as usual,' Anna murmured. She laid her head down gently on the dog's bony skull. They breathed quietly. Together for a little longer.

James came into the room carrying a large hold-all. He dropped it on the floor and slumped into a chair. He stared morosely through the windows at the dripping magnolia trees.

'We should have left sooner,' he said. 'When the UN first started the evacuation. The Hamiltons packed up everything and got out as soon as the war started. We should have done the same.'

'The Hamiltons were a different type of people.' Marie Carter entered the room backwards, dragging a heavy packing case along the floor.

'What are you doing with that, Mum?' Anna asked.

'I've packed some useful stuff in it. When we're settled in Kenya Joseph might be able to send it. Perhaps they'll leave this house alone as it's on the compound.'

Yet another lie. Everyone was lying to everyone else. It was easier than facing the truth. They knew they would lose everything. As soon as word got out that the United Nations troops had gone, the houses would be stripped bare by a whooping, drunken, gun-toting rabble, on the hospital compound or not. Then the looters would strip the hospital. Steal the food and the drugs and the blankets. Steal the very bedframes and mattresses from under the patients and leave the sick to heal themselves, or not, upon the floor.

'The Hamiltons were only here three years, not twenty. They didn't have much to pack. And they didn't have the same commitment. They just walked out on their patients. You wouldn't have wanted your father to do that. Doctors can't just run away like that.'

'They were young. Their children were just babies,' said Jonathon Carter, picking up his pen and resuming his final instructions for the Rwandan doctor who would take over from him until the hospital was evacuated. 'Inexperienced. Appalled by the way the Hutu and Tutsi were treating each other, and very, very frightened. You can't blame them for that. We've all got used to the brutality of Rwanda.'

'I haven't got used to it,' Anna said. 'I don't think I'll ever get used to it.'

'Perhaps not, but we have to accept it. The Hutu and Tutsi have been at each others' throats for centuries. Nothing is going to change that. The Hamiltons simply couldn't come to terms with what happens here. They did what they had to do. I did what I had to do.'

'Yes,' James muttered. 'But the result is the same. All you did was keep things going for a few more months. By next week the hospital will be empty. Staying made no difference.'

'It was a family decision to stay, James, if you remember,' Anna protested. 'We *all* decided to hang on and see what happened.'

'I know,' said James. 'And now we're probably the only non-Rwandans left. Joseph says this last shuttle tonight is mainly for Rwandan politicians. Rats deserting sinking ships. Many of the ones running

3

out are the ones responsible for the mess. Now they're going to sit in safety in Nairobi and let things here take their course.'

BRRRNNNNG! BRRRNNNNG!

The sudden noise of the phone ringing startled them.

Anna and James looked at each other, each knowing that this was the moment.

'Doctor Carter speaking ... yes ... yes ... I understand ... yes, got it. Thank you, Major.' He put the telephone down. 'That was Major Cartier Bresson. The helicopters are coming in over the lake now. They'll be here in half an hour or so.'

'Right. That's it then.' Anna crossed the room and picked up her bag. It seemed very small. She thought of all the things she was leaving behind, things she would never see again. All the accumulations of her fifteen years of life. All her memories.

She shrugged. *Only things*, she thought. 'Right, I'm ready,' she said out loud.

Jonathon Carter got up from his desk. 'The major says we're to take the outer road, through the shanty town. The Tutsi rebels have taken the main parts of town, round the radio station. The UN have secured the airport. They're pulling out all their remaining troops tonight too.'

Anna put her hand gently on Alfred's head and patted him.

'No tears,' ordered Marie Carter.

'Bye, Alfred,' Anna whispered.

'And don't look back,' said James. 'No one look back.'

They walked out of the front door, closing it behind

4

them. As they walked away they heard Alfred whining pathetically. Then they climbed into the Range Rover and pulled away. The armed *askari* at the main entrance to the compound saw them coming and swung the gate open.

The Range Rover swept out on to the road.

It seemed like the end of the world, that twenty-minute journey down to Kigali.

But it wasn't.

The end of their world was only just beginning.

Two

'*Hooooo–tooooo.*'

The boy shivered.

Somewhere, in another part of the town, gunfire rattled.

A scream.

Whoops of laughter. Mindless laughter. The empty cackle of the madman.

And then again, the voice, drawn out, mocking.

'*Hooooo . . . tooooo.*'

Somewhere, down the street, a door slammed. Its glass fell out and shattered on the concrete step.

Another crazed whoop.

More laughter. Not one man. Several.

Gunshots again. Closer.

'It's all right,' he whispered to himself. 'They'll go by. They won't find me.'

They will though. They're thorough. They'll tear the house apart. Plank by plank.

'HUTU.'

This time it was barked sharply, cracking through the heavy air.

Another voice followed it. Mocking, gloating, singsong.

'Come out. Come out.'

Thud.

The first footfall on the steps of the house.

Now he could hear a man breathing.

And smell him. The smell of sweat and oil and guns and vengeance.

He tried to squeeze back, further under the bed, further into the dark.

Thud.

The second step.

The boy began to tremble violently.

This was the end. There was no escape now.

And then . . . another sound.

Faint. Distant. Slow.

Wap-wap . . . wap-wap . . . wap-wap . . . wap-wap.

The low, distant, rhythmic *thwack* of great, metal blades scything through water-laden air.

The helicopters.

Helicopters in convoy, heading in towards the town, to the airport.

Back from the Nairobi shuttle. A swarm of them, like great, armoured bees.

The feet paused.

A grunt of annoyance. Barked orders.

And the feet began to move away, hurriedly.

Bright light swept past the house window, briefly lighting up the inside of the room. He readied himself to run.

The helicopters roared in over the town, their searchlights washing the streets with swift, swirling brushstrokes of white light.

The thud of feet faded away as the Tutsi ran into hiding, fearful of the cannon and the rockets and the eager fingers on the buttons.

Now.

The boy scrambled out from under the bed, rolled

on to his feet and ran to the door. Lights were moving down the street, swinging from side to side. Looking up he could see the underbellies of the great machines as they drummed slowly past.

He waited until the lights were past, then swung the door open and hurled himself down the steps on to the road.

And ran. The houses echoed his footsteps back to him.

'*Hutu, hutu, hutu,*' his feet seemed to chant as they slapped the wet earth.

The lights of the helicopters faded into the distance.

'*Hooooooo-tooooooo,*' moaned the wind rushing past his ears.

Wap-wap . . . wap-wap . . . wap-wap.

A lone helicopter, a straggler, sank down from the night clouds and swept past above him. Its lights briefly illuminated him. Betrayed him to watchers.

Run.

Run for your life.

The Tutsi soldiers emerged from hiding.

'Follow him,' their commander snarled.

He spat on the ground.

'Find him. And bring him to me.'

8

Three

Darkness falls quickly in the tropics. The short journey down into the town was a journey into blackness. What lights they had been able to see dotted about the town as they crept down the hill had been from fires. Some innocent, cooking fires only, but some not. Otherwise there was little light. The electricity supply had been sporadic for months. Darkness suited everyone's purpose.

'The streets are very quiet,' Jonathon Carter remarked as they entered the town. 'Ominously so.'

'Try the radio,' suggested Anna. 'See if they're on air. We might get some idea what's happening.'

But the radio gave out only a monotonous, pulsating hiss. Whoever had made the last broadcast hadn't bothered to switch off, or had fled, or worse. Behind the hiss the sounds from the building and from the surrounding streets were being picked up by the microphones and transmitted. Faint sounds, but chilling. Of guns and breakage and angry voices and fear. The soundtrack of chaos. Of a country losing control.

Jonathon Carter slowed the vehicle down.

'Why are you slowing?' James asked.

'Lights. I can see lights in the sky. There. Coming in over the hills to the south.'

'The helicopters,' Marie Carter exclaimed.

Jonathon Carter started to accelerate again. 'They'll be on the ground in a few minutes.' He swung the vehicle into Kamuzinzi Street and accelerated hard down the hill.

Ahead of them, clearly visible, the helicopters were coming in to land. They slowed and tilted majestically back on their haunches as they made their final approach. The great machines exuded safety. Protected by them, cocooned in them, their great searchlights making day of dense tropical night, what harm could come to you?

'What a wonderful sight,' whispered Marie Carter. 'But I never thought I would leave here, my country, my *home*, in such terrible circumstances.'

'Don't think about it,' her husband replied.

'Don't think about anything,' said James. 'And, above all, don't count chickens. We're not there yet. Just drive. Just get there, fast.'

'Not far now. Just into Mikeno Street, then it's a straight run.'

He swung the Range Rover round the corner and accelerated down the final approach to the airport.

Immediately it became clear why the streets had seemed so quiet. Hundreds, perhaps thousands, of people were gathered around the boundary, frantic with fear, their children clinging to them, their possessions wrapped in bright sheets carried on their backs. Pathetically unaware that these helicopters were not for them, that there was no escape for them, they clamoured at the gates and fences, wailing and crying and imploring, shouting with anger, shouting with terror.

A phalanx of about thirty UN Land Rovers

10

blocked the main entrance. A line of soldiers wearing light blue berets and holding automatic weapons in their hands stood behind the vehicles.

Jonathon Carter slowed the Range Rover down and flashed the headlights several times as they approached.

Immediately one of the Land Rovers pulled out and headed towards them. It turned in the road directly in front of them, halting them. An armed soldier jumped out and came over.

'Identification?' he demanded, peering in through the window.

'Doctor Jonathon Carter and family. Here are our papers.'

The soldier nodded. 'Right. Follow us.'

The Land Rover drove straight at the milling crowd, parting it. The Range Rover followed through. Angry fists hammered its sides.

They were led through a phalanx of armed soldiers to the side of the airport and through a gate where a tank sat at battle readiness, its gun pointing out towards the town.

The helicopters were now on the ground, their engines roaring and their rotors whirling in readiness for instant flight. The noise was deafening, disorientating. The privileged passengers, the chosen ones, milled around, confused, waiting to be given instructions. UN officers moved among them handing out cards with numbers on them. Seeing the Range Rover, one of them ran across and handed boarding papers to Jonathon Carter.

'Helicopter Five, quickly!' he shouted.

'Right.'

They climbed out and began to hurry towards the helicopters.

'Can you see which it is?' Anna asked.

Bright searchlights swept this way and that, blinding them.

'Not yet.'

'There,' said James. 'Second one from the left.'

They headed towards it.

Briefly, from behind them, there was a burst of gunfire. The UN officers looked back anxiously across the airstrip to the terminal building.

'Come on,' said one of them.

Four

He kept to the side streets where darkness was his ally.

He moved quickly but silently, terrified his feet would betray him. He knew the rebel Tutsi would be following him and would show no mercy, as they had shown none to his father and mother.

He wept inwardly for them. They had remained to the end, hoping some order could be restored. Hung on when friends, advisers, the senior men of government had abandoned them and fled to Nairobi. Hung on until there was no further hope.

Even today, finally, when they had decided that the Tutsi were unstoppable and there was nothing to do but go, even then his father had been let down. His own guard, the best the army had, those picked by the generals to escort them to the airport, had vanished, melted away into the shadows when they saw the rebels converging on the house. So his father and mother had died in a hail of bullets, knowing that their own people, people of the same Hutu blood, had not, in the end, been willing to fight for them.

Now he was alone. And unless he made it to the helicopters, his own death was certain.

He turned into the narrow back street behind Mikeno Street. He could hear the noise from the airport. Not just the helicopter engines but the people clamouring to escape. He had little time. The helicopters would only be on the ground a short while.

He ran again, time more important than concealment, and eventually emerged on to the airport forecourt.

Hundreds of people had converged around the airport gate, shouting at the line of UN soldiers, pleading with them, offering them bribes. The soldiers were stony-faced. Very few people were being allowed through.

He glanced nervously around. Hutu soldiers, ordered to back up the UN, were gathered in frightened groups.

He decided he would not go to them. They were not reliable. Fleeing Hutu had been casting off their uniforms and Tutsi donning them as a disguise.

He pushed his way slowly through the crowds. People tried to impede him, push him back. Sometimes he had to drop to his knees and push through their legs.

Eventually he got to the front and scrambled up to a UN soldier.

'I am Dominic Seregera. I am to be taken out tonight to Nairobi.'

'Papers?'

'I have no papers. I had to run away and leave them behind.'

'No papers, no entry.'

'You don't understand. I am Dominic Seregera. My father is President Gregoire Seregera. The Tutsi have killed him. My mother too. There is a place for me on the helicopter.'

The soldier looked him up and down.

14

'The president's son, eh?' His voice was heavy with sarcasm. 'And I'm the President of the USA. Get back over there with everyone else.' He pushed Dominic in the chest with his gun, sending him reeling back into the crowd. He fell heavily. Feet trampled him.

Dominic scrambled out again and looked around wildly. He thought he saw now, joining the crowd at the back, the distinctive camouflage caps of the Tutsi rebels. They had followed him. He looked again at the UN guards. They would never believe him. He glanced back into the crowd. They *were* Tutsi. Unless he could somehow make it on to a helicopter he was doomed. They would drag him away and kill him just because of who he was.

He hunched down, desperate to hide himself in the crowd.

Five

Just who had fired the shots wasn't clear. Perhaps it was an accident, a nervous finger twitching unintentionally on a trigger. Perhaps it was one of the UN soldiers firing into the air to warn the crowds to keep back.

There was a moment of stunned silence. Then all control was lost. A great cry rose up, so loud it could clearly be heard above the roar of the engines. And the crowd surged forward. They surrounded the phalanx of Land Rovers and overturned them. The UN soldiers readied themselves to fire. The mob, terrified beyond reason, rushed the fences, smashing them down, trampling people into them, crushing them underfoot. A huge swell of people swept into the airport and began to surge towards the helicopters. Dominic found himself swept, helpless, along with them.

There was more gunfire as the UN soldiers emerged from the concourse on to the airstrip and tried to establish some control. First they fired into the air, then low over the heads of the crowd. It did no good. For those who knew that to remain in Rwanda meant death, bullets held little fear now. A bullet now or a bullet later, what was the difference? The helicopters were their only chance. They rushed the soldiers, knocking them aside. Guards from all round the perimeter fence rushed in to try to stop the mob, to no avail.

Round by the side gate, where the Carters had entered, the tank turned and pointed its gun inwards.

A UN officer appeared by the Carters' side.

'Quickly,' he ordered. 'Run. Take any helicopter. Any you can get in.'

The mob was approaching rapidly. A maelstrom of humanity.

Then everything became confusion. Soldiers appeared in front of them and the pilots, seeing what was happening, started to lift their helicopters off the ground in readiness. More soldiers appeared at their sides, grabbed them by the arms and hustled them along. The sound of the mob grew behind them and caught up with them. Suddenly they found themselves being carried along in a sea of people. James grabbed Anna's hand. Fleetingly they glimpsed their mother and father being swept away from them in the crowd.

At the perimeter gate, two Tutsi militia men climbed on to the tank and silently opened its hatch. Seconds later the bodies of the UN tank crew were dumped outside.

'Where's Mum and Dad?' Anna shouted, looking around wildly.

'They'll be all right,' a soldier yelled. 'They'll be going for another helicopter. Just run.'

The wind from the rotors was pushing them back now. They were close to one of the great machines. A hatch in the side gaped and a crewman beckoned. They were pushed and hauled inside where they collapsed, breathless.

And a Tutsi settled himself into the gunner's seat

of the tank and surveyed the controls. The gun raised
slightly under his touch. He took a sighting.

'Get down that end,' the crewman shouted at James
and Anna. 'Make room.'

They scuttled along the floor, towards the front.
The noise and the vibration were immense.

More people were shoved and pulled in. And more
and more. No one knew now who should be here and
who not. More gunfire rattled out as the last of the
UN peacekeepers cleared the mob away from the
helicopters so they could board themselves. Engines
screamed up to full power as some of the helicopters
were filled and soared up into the night sky.

And finally James and Anna's helicopter was full.
The engine note increased and they began to rise.

They were no more than ten metres off the ground
when a shell from the tank hit the rear rotor blades.
There was a tremendous bang as the rotor ripped
itself off the tail. The helicopter lurched briefly under
the impact. Then it became uncontrollable. Ponder-
ously slowly, it spun twice completely round, its
engine screaming then, with a bone-breaking thump,
crashed back down on to the ground. For a minute
or two it shuddered with such violence it threatened
to tear itself into pieces. James and Anna clutched
each other in fear. Slowly the shaking subsided.

For a while there was shocked incomprehension.
Then there was smoke, thick acrid smoke. Someone
kicked open the hatch and people started climbing
over each other to escape, panic making them fight
each other to reach the door first.

'Come on,' said James. He grasped Anna's hand
and they crawled in the other direction, towards the

cockpit. The pilot was slumped forward in his seat, blocking the door. Blood ran from a deep gash on his head. He was conscious but his eyes were glazed. James leaned past him, kicked open the door and climbed across him. He jumped down on to the tarmac then turned and grasped the pilot by the arm.

'Quickly, Anna, help me get him out,' he shouted.

Anna grasped the pilot's other arm and tried to push him towards the door. But he was a dead weight.

'Hurry,' she shouted at him, pushing with all her strength. 'Help yourself. Get out.'

He turned his blood-spattered face towards her and stared blankly, uncomprehending.

Then Anna felt her shoulders grasped by strong hands.

'Go,' said a voice. And she was pushed past the pilot into the doorway and into James's waiting arms. He dragged her out.

'Run,' shouted the soldier who had pushed her. 'Get away. We'll look after him. Save yourselves.'

They turned and fled as fast they could, away from the stricken machine, away into the darkness. Overhead they could see the lights and hear the engines of the departing helicopters. The lucky ones.

Behind them there were shouts and screams as the angry mob closed in upon the wreck, seeking vengeance on the passengers, the deserters who were leaving them behind.

James and Anna collapsed beside the ruined fence. It was very dark now the helicopters' lights were gone. Dismayed, they sat in white-faced silence, hugging each other to slow their trembling.

Anna felt something warm and wet running down

her face. She put her hand to her head and found a deep gash above her eye.

'I'm bleeding,' she said to James.

'Me too. I took the skin off my legs getting out of the cockpit.'

Back across the airport, gunfire sounded. It went on for a long time.

Neither James nor Anna spoke for many minutes. But their brains whirled. Their mother and father were gone. Violence and mayhem confronted them across the airport. They were hurt, mortally afraid for their parents' safety and their own, stranded and vulnerable. No words could be found.

Anna wept silently. James fought back his tears and held her tightly.

By the gate, the tank's engine roared. Its metal tracks screeched on the tarmac as it spun round and headed out into town, bent on havoc. Anna lifted her head and watched it go.

The Range Rover, she noticed, was still where they had left it.

'James,' she said, pointing.

The mob was dispersing. Hope gone, people were fleeing in terror. There was nobody near the Range Rover.

'Keep to the shadows,' said Anna, as they hurriedly made their way to the vehicle.

The keys were still in the ignition. 'Thank God for that,' breathed James as he turned it.

Six

As the helicopters rose, the town descended into chaos. Vehicles screeched and roared up and down the streets, the abandoned Land Rovers of the United Nations had been rolled upright and were now filled with grim-faced men intent on vengeance or looting or escape. Uproar reigned. Hutu soldiers threw away their uniforms, stopped civilians at gunpoint and stole their clothes. Tutsi searched for Hutu. Hutu lurked in doorways waiting to shoot Tutsi. Women and children tried to stay out of the way of both, or slyly joined in with machetes or knives.

And, as James negotiated the Range Rover out on to the road, the enormity of what had happened began to sink in: they were alone in what had now become perhaps the most dangerous place on earth.

'Turn left,' Anna suggested after a time. 'Go out through the factory area. There won't be many people there.'

'Right.' James accelerated into the darkness. 'I hope Mum and Dad make it.'

'All the other helicopters seemed to get away. They'll be well on their way to Nairobi now.'

'They'll be frantic with worry,' James observed quietly. 'They won't know whether we're dead or alive.'

A pick-up hurtled out of a side street and turned

21

in front of them. Its tyres screamed. James braked hard. Briefly they glimpsed armed men in the back of the vehicle. It shot away, ignoring them, its occupants intent upon their own evil.

'We're lucky we *are* alive. The rest of them weren't as fast as us. If we hadn't got out at the front we'd have been trapped by the mob.'

Anna nodded. The fate of the other occupants of the helicopter was beyond imagination.

They drove through the dark bulks of the factories in the industrial area.

'Do we have a plan?' Anna asked, eventually.

'Only to get out of town and to somewhere safer.'

'Go home again, first,' Anna suggested. 'See what's happening. Perhaps we'll have time to think there.'

As soon as they could they pulled off the sealed roads on to the loggers' track which snaked up through the forest on to the ridge to the north of the town. Occasionally, as they negotiated the ridge, the forest thinned and, from perilous height, they could catch brief glimpses of the town. James stopped the vehicle at the highest point and they looked out over Kigali's densely packed houses and shanties. They sat in silence, sadly thinking of the better times when people would come up here at nightfall and sit and watch the spectacle of the lights coming on in the town and the cooking fires springing up in gardens as meals were cooked on open fires.

There were fires tonight too. Big fires. The sound of gunfire, faint, unreal, floated up to them. Flashes of orange and scarlet, like giant fireworks, burst here and there, the soft thud of explosion following seconds behind.

James shook his head in disbelief.

'The town's tearing itself apart.'

'Now the UN's gone,' Anna said, 'there's nothing to stop them.'

In truth there hadn't been much before, but there had been *something*, some small control. But the troops were gone, the politicians gone, and the last, flimsy thread of restraint gone with them. Now the vengeful and the criminal and the mad were unleashed upon each other.

'That looks like it's the Catholic Mission on fire, there on the Boulevard de l'OUA. Can you see?' whispered Anna. 'Why would they do that? Only good came out of there.'

'The priests all left. Nobody's been there for weeks.'

'That's not the point. Why burn it down?'

'Why do they do anything?' James sighed. He put the car into gear again. 'We've seen enough.'

He started to pull away.

'More than enough,' Anna agreed.

But there was more to come.

The main track passed across the ridge about a hundred metres above the hospital. A narrow service track ran from that down to a part of the grounds where only the engineers and maintenance staff ever went. A quiet, dark corner normally, away from the hustle and bustle of hospital life.

Tonight it was dimly, patchily illuminated by the flames of the burning hospital filtering through the trees.

The Range Rover slid quietly in through the gate and came to a stop.

From where they were they could see round the

boiler-houses. Could see, brokenly through the trees, the outline of burning buildings, flames licking from windows, sparks shooting up into the night sky. Could see the driveway down to the main gate, towards which vague human shapes, some on crutches, some crawling, some pushing wheelchairs, limped and struggled, backlit by fire. A long, sad line of the sick and the injured, the desperate and the frightened, fleeing the mayhem of the conflagration.

Across the drive, against the hillside, the lights were on in all the staff houses. In *their* house. Sounds of shouting and breaking glass drifted across to them and shadowy figures passed across windows.

There was a long silence.

'It was all over anyway,' Anna whispered eventually. 'We were only pretending. We all knew it was over.'

'Yes,' said James, 'we knew.'

'Mad.' Anna shook her head in disbelief. 'They've gone completely mad. Burning the hospital. What can that possibly achieve?'

'No doubt it's a symbol of colonial domination,' James said bitterly. 'Forty years after Independence. Or perhaps it's Hutu burning it down because too many Tutsi were treated there. Or the other way round. Or perhaps it's just the local thugs having a night on the town. Frankly I don't care what the reason is. I don't care what they do now, so long as they don't come near us. Everything's ended. The sooner we get away from here the better.'

'And go where?'

'I've no idea yet.'

'Maybe we could wait here until they've gone,'

Anna suggested, 'then creep back into the house. Hole up there until we gather our senses.'

'They won't leave the house standing, Anna. They'll burn that too. When they've finished looting it, they'll torch it. They don't do jobs by halves.'

James was right of course.

There was another long silence as they sat, their previous lives flickering across their minds like the flames which would inevitably consume them.

'How much petrol in the tank?' Anna asked eventually.

'Not much. It's under a quarter full. Twenty-five litres perhaps. Ninety kilometres at most. What are you thinking? Making our way down to Burundi?'

'No, Burundi's in nearly as big a mess as Rwanda. But you're right, I was thinking of escape routes. I expect you were too.'

James nodded.

'And?'

'And I came to the conclusion that every border will be closed very quickly now.'

'So did I,' Anna agreed. 'But they'll concentrate on the main ones. The Uganda one at Kidaho will be the last.'

James turned and looked at her. 'Why do you think that?'

'Because no one uses it much any more except people sneaking across to do some illegal shopping. And the border guards don't care much about that because they're too busy joining in. Everyone trying to escape the country will use the new road that goes from Kigali to Kabale. It's sealed all the way. A very fast road.'

25

'Hmm,' James said. 'You're right. I remember when I went on the trip to Ruwenzori a few years ago with the climbing club we went the way you're suggesting. Out to Ruhengeri, then to Kidaho and into Uganda at Cyanika. We didn't even get our passports checked.'

'Will we have enough petrol? Ruhengeri to the border is . . . what . . . about thirty-five kilometres?'

'About,' James agreed.

'We wouldn't make it then. Here to Ruhengeri is at least eighty. We'd find ourselves stranded with about twenty kilometres still to go.'

'We're stranded wherever we are,' observed James, logically. 'Is it worse to be stranded at Ruhengeri than here?'

'No, much better probably. Nothing could be worse than Kigali now. Anyway there'll be petrol in the store here.' Anna pointed to the square out-building attached to the wall of the boiler house.

'We'll need food too,' said James. 'Enough for a day or two.' He opened the door, climbed out and studied the burning buildings closely. 'The fire hasn't spread too far yet. And the looters are busy over at the houses. If I sneak in the back way I could get some food from the hospital kitchens.'

'I'll come with you,' Anna said. 'We could do with some bandages and medical stuff in case our cuts go septic. If I can get through to Dad's office he's got a secret stash there.'

They made their way across to the hospital, keeping to the trees and the shadows. The roaring from the burning building grew louder as they approached. The main administration block was well alight and flames were beginning to spread to the part of the hospital where the wards and operating theatre were. Patients were crying out and screaming and hospital porters, gardeners, cooks, all the able-bodied were desperately trying to carry the bedridden and infirm to safety.

In the mêlée James and Anna went unnoticed. They slipped into the building at the back door by the kitchens.

'I'll see you back at the Range Rover,' Anna whispered, as James disappeared into the kitchen.

'Take care,' called James, already opening cupboards.

Anna headed down the corridor towards her father's office. The electricity was off but the pale emergency lighting gave enough light to see by. She noticed the operating-theatre doors were wide open and the equipment scattered and broken.

She tried to shut her ears to the cries of distress from the wards at the far end of the corridor.

She reached her father's office and went in. There was less light here and it was difficult to see, but she knew her father kept a torch in his desk drawer ready for power failures. She found it and switched it on. Smoke was seeping into the room from the ceiling as fire spread through the roof. She would need to hurry. She crossed to the filing cabinet, put her shoulder against it and pushed it away from the wall. Then she knelt and lifted a floorboard to reveal the stash of drugs her father kept hidden. She selected some antibiotic powder to treat their cuts and an assortment of antibiotic pills. She threw them into a paper sick-bag, swept some bandages and sticking plasters into it from a shelf and turned to leave.

She reeled back with shock. Leaning against the doorpost, teeth shining in a leering smile, a rebel soldier regarded her. She gasped in dismay. She hadn't heard a sound.

The soldier laughed softly. A menacing laugh. Anna noticed he had a bottle in his hand.

He lurched into the room. She looked round frantically for something to defend herself with. She could see nothing. He reached out towards her and staggered. His eyes rolled around in his head. Anna realized he was so drunk he could barely stand. Perhaps she could avoid him.

She tried to duck under his arm and make for the door, but he was quicker than she had expected. She got past him but he spun quickly. She felt his hand grab the collar of her blouse at the back of her neck. He grunted and staggered. She felt sudden nausea at the smell of whiskey from his breath. She struggled hard, but he was too strong. He started to drag her back into the room.

'James,' she yelled at the top of her voice. But she knew he was too far away to hear.

Then suddenly a dark shape hurtled through the doorway and into the room. Anna heard a deep, throaty growl and the shape threw itself at the arm which was imprisoning her. Alfred. The soldier screamed as ferocious teeth locked in his flesh. His grip released immediately and Anna ran for the door. She turned into the corridor and fled for her life.

James was just coming out of the kitchens as she ran past.

'Whoa,' he said. 'What's the matter?'

'I'll tell you later. Just get out of here. Now.'

Together they ran back to the Range Rover. Anna climbed into the passenger seat and sat trembling.

'That,' said James, when Anna had gasped the story out, 'was a very narrow escape. Sit here while I get the petrol. I got the storeroom key from the care-taker's room.'

The fire was spreading rapidly. The looters were torching the houses. Anna could see flames beginning to lick the windows of their house. Their lives were vanishing in violence and smoke.

And then Alfred arrived. There was a brief rustling, then a scrabbling and scraping at the door and the ridgeback climbed in through the window.

Anna grunted as the dog landed on her knee and nuzzled his slobbering mouth into her neck.

'Oh,' Anna gasped, pushing him away. He snuggled on to the seat beside her. She put her arm round the ridgeback's neck. His tongue rasped her hand.

She hugged the dog's head. 'I might have known you'd be there to save me.'

Alfred wagged his tail and whined appreciatively.

James reappeared carrying two red jerry-cans. Alfred jumped out of the window and went to greet him.

'Thought you might turn up,' James said, smiling affectionately. He went to the back of the Range Rover, put the cans down on the floor and put his hand on the tailgate catch.

Alfred began to growl menacingly.

'What's the matter?' James asked, looking around nervously. He saw nothing to account for Alfred's warning.

The ridgeback snarled again, staring at the tailgate, then began to bark with great ferocity.

James realized what he was being told. He reacted instantly. He ran to the passenger door, flung it open and hauled an astonished Anna out.

'Away from the car, quickly. There's someone in the back. Someone's got in while we were away.'

They were about to run away when a voice spoke to them from the back of the Range Rover.

'Wait. Please. It's all right. I'll explain.'

A dark shape rose up from among the bags.

'Please. Call the dog off. I'll explain.'

James and Anna peered in. They found themselves looking at the frightened face of a teenage Rwandan boy.

'What on earth . . .?' Anna exclaimed.

'Alfred,' James ordered. 'Stop it. Sit.'

The dog's fearsome snarling faded away to disappointed whines.

James opened the tailgate and the boy climbed out.

'Who, in heaven's name,' James asked in astonishment, 'are you?'

'And what are you doing in our car?' Anna asked.

'My name,' said the boy, 'is Dominic Seregera.'

Dominic sat in the back of the Range Rover guarded by Alfred, who stared at him with great suspicion. As they sped away Dominic explained his plight. Anna and James exchanged glances. Rwanda was not an easy place to trust anybody. Was this boy who he said he was? And if he was, were they not in even greater danger by assisting him?

'How did you go on about getting food?' Anna enquired of James eventually, to break a long silence.

'I got plenty of rice and some packets of those awful hard biscuits that break your teeth. That's about all there was. How did you do?'

'I got bandages and some antibiotics.'

They started to pull away. Anna glanced again at the hospital.

'Do you think they'll all get out?' she asked.

'They're helping each other as best they can. Though where they're going or what awaits them, goodness only knows. There'll be no place of safety anywhere now.'

The Range Rover pulled out through the gate on to the track. At the ridge they paused briefly once more to look down on Kigali. The fires had spread. It seemed now the whole town was on fire. They sat for a moment with their memories.

Then they turned their backs on their past.

Seven

The group started to stir just after dawn.

They rustled in their night-nests and peered out into the cold morning mists. The rainforest dripped gently down on to them and as they sat up they brushed the moisture off their black fur.

An infant chattered and mewled, asking to be fed. Its mother grumbled into wakefulness. One of the older females admonished her with an irritable snarl and others growled agreement. Grunts and scratchings and sighs emanated from various points of the sleeping site.

The old silverback lay listening to the noises. He yawned loudly, his great mouth opening to reveal massive canines, yellow with age. An infant, hearing the yawn, came over to inspect him. She kept a respectful distance, peered at him for a moment or two, then peeled her lips back over her teeth, chattered cheekily at him, turned and executed a forward somersault inviting him to play.

He growled. He was in no mood to play yet. He was rarely, these days, in the mood to play.

The infant's knuckles plunged down on to the ground again at the warning. She paused briefly then, either in defiance or sheer high spirits, did a backwards flip, dashed away, shot up a tree, rattled through its branches, swung across into the next one and skittered down it on to the ground again. Then she returned to her mother, chuckling.

The silverback yawned again, stretched and groaned. Sometimes he was very tired. Sometimes the night chill made it hard for him to rise in the mornings. His bones would be stiff and his joints painful when he moved. Old injuries from past battles would come back to haunt him. He would ache. New injuries would take weeks to heal. So, most days now, he would lie in his soft night-nest of leaves and moss until the sun seeped through the trees, lifted the cold of the dawn mists and warmed him through. Occasionally he would not rise until hunger forced him to.

Now too, the daily routine wearied him. The constant vigilance, the constant listening for danger, the constant search for new feeding grounds.

But that was something he would never be able to relinquish. The responsibility for the well-being of the group would always be his. Now and then one of the blackbacks, approaching maturity, or a young silverback, the spine just beginning to grey, would challenge him. Prance and display and growl. But it was always hollow and they all knew it. A fight of sorts might ensue, but a sound cuff to the head or a swift bite to the shoulder would settle matters.

He still had all his strength and authority.

Well, *almost*. Could *summon* all his strength.

For the moment.

The glory days were gone though, his instincts told him that. The females made up to the blackbacks now, not him. The new generations being born were not his blood any more. And they were few and sickly. Often now the whole group was hungry for days. The competition for food was fierce, fights would break out, the strongest would win. The females were not the strongest. They would be the first to become thin. And their offspring, when born, would be frail and would not survive. Gradually the group was becoming smaller and smaller and it could no longer challenge the more powerful groups for feeding rights.

Yes, the good days were gone.

But the men . . . they were not gone, would never go.

Of all the trials of daily living the men were the worst, their presence the most pernicious. And their presence was everywhere even when they themselves were not. They left danger wherever they went. This was the most tiring thing of all. No movement could be made, no step taken anywhere in the forest without vigilance, no path followed without looking for the signs. Looking for the patch of vegetation on the forest floor that was not quite the colour or the texture it should be, and skirting round it, shepherding the group, knowing that the men had dug a pit and spiked it. Looking up for the vine that did not hang just right, that was angled and fastened high and held a heavy log in balance, ready to fall and crush whoever tripped the wire concealed on the path. Watching for the curved bamboo or tree, the one bent over and anchored to the ground. The one that, if you stepped into the trap, would snap upright and haul you into the air by the cruel wire round your ankle and leave you there until you starved.

And the constant listening for their voices, their

guns, their footsteps or their dogs. And sniffing the air for the smell of them, of sweat and malevolence and tobacco and woodsmoke.

The hated men, fear and death their only bequest to the forest and its inhabitants.

And yet . . .

Deep in his mind, from a lifetime ago, there remained a sense of a time when man was not a threat to him. A time when there had been trust. Dimmed by years, without distinct form, it was not so much a memory as a feeling that there should *be* one. A feeling which would nag him and make him go and seek the places again, because to see them would clear a little of the mind's mist.

And, when he arrived there, he would sit in the forest watching and waiting, just as he had waited before, all those years ago. Not waiting *for* anything, just waiting now because he had waited then.

That was what was clearest. The waiting, so long ago.

He had returned to his own kind, of course. Eventually. Though for days, many, many days he had sat waiting, not knowing what he waited for. Just knowing that things were changed and that her voice no longer spoke to him and that because she did not speak he did not know what to do and was fearful and confused.

In the end hunger moved him on. The vines and thistles, nettles and celery close by were soon consumed, so he had no choice but to go back to the others, to find their feeding ground and rejoin them and be where she had taken him and wanted him to be. Where he too knew he should be. For, although with her there was a bond that could never be broken, she was not the same as he and the pull of blood, of species, would always have been irresistible. And, back with his own kind, gradually time passed and the pull of her became less and the memory limped to the back of his mind. Not lost, displaced by the recurring urgencies of food and rest and finding safety and living and growing. Of being what he was.

Now, in age, the feeling returned more frequently than before; would call him and pull him back to this place. For a while, a day and a night perhaps, he would simply sit in the dank wetness of the forest shadows, close to the cabin, until the sheen of silver droplets from the forest rain penetrated his thick black fur and the dawn cold and hunger would drive him away again. And now and then he would beat his chest and cry out. A cry so deep and booming that the trees would shudder as though a momentary breeze rattled their leaves. A cry of such great, cavernous resonance that it would carry through miles of the densest forest on earth, scattering cackling vervet monkeys into the highest branches, sending the timid bushbuck diving for cover and the forest pigs scuttling in furious circles.

OOOOOM-AAAAAAGH.
OOOOOM-AAAAAAGH.

Hollow and lonely, the great gorilla's cry would roll down the sodden mountain slopes. And the village people below would look up, peer into the impenetrable pall of mist, of *mystery*, shrouding the high slopes and shake their heads.

'Ah,' they would murmur. '*Huzuni. Huzuni.*'

The sad one.

Eight

James opened the lid of the cubby box between the Range Rover's front seats, took out a small screwdriver and began to remove the screws securing the box's inner lining. He eventually pulled it out and turned it over. Taped to its underside was an envelope which he tore open to reveal a bundle of US dollar bills.

'Our father's emergency store,' he explained. 'The key to many doors.'

Dominic looked doubtful. 'Dollars won't help me if anyone recognizes me.'

'Is anyone likely to recognize you?' Anna asked. 'I didn't even know the president had a son. And I've lived here all my life.'

'My face is known to some. I tried to stay in the background. My father said it was better.'

'I'm sorry for what happened to your parents,' Anna said.

'I will revenge them perhaps, in the future. The Tutsi are rising to the top now. But one day they will pay. Today it is their turn. It will be our turn again.'

James and Anna looked at each other. The endless cycle of Tutsi–Hutu violence was baffling, the hatreds incomprehensible.

Dominic noticed the glance. 'I don't expect you to understand,' he said. 'Most of the people themselves don't understand. They just know that the BaHutu and WaTutsi have always been enemies. Once, I suppose, there were reasons. Land and power. Those are forgotten, but things have been done which can never be forgotten. Terrible things. Now we are born hating each other. The sun rises in the morning and sets at night. And Hutu and Tutsi kill each other. That's the order of things.'

Anna shook her head sadly. 'It's such a waste.'

'Yes,' said Dominic simply.

'It's getting light,' James said. 'Let's go.'

Negotiating a border is often perilous in Africa. In some places just wanting to cross a border at all is, in the eyes of the authorities, a suspicious activity. In normal times things would always be smoothed by bribes, but these were not normal times. Anything could happen.

So, as the Range Rover crept up to the miserable collection of huts and the steel-pole barrier which marks the end of Rwandan territory and the beginning of three kilometres of no man's land stretching out to the Ugandan border at Cyanika, they were all very nervous.

Although less than an hour after dawn, the mist was lifting and the air beginning to load itself with the threat of heat. Already a line of about a dozen cars and pick-up trucks waited at the barrier. Early-starters perhaps or, more likely, unfortunates who had been there all night, trapped by the dusk curfew; or longer, kept waiting interminably at the whim of corrupt officials. Disconsolate-looking people milled about aimlessly or sat dejectedly on the ground or slept with their backs against the wheels of their vehicles, allowing time to pass. People who had learned long ago that any attempt to speed things up would be regarded as insolence, punishable by more days of waiting as they worked their way up from the back of the queue again.

At the head of the line of vehicles an Asian merchant with a pick-up truck full of carvings was arguing fiercely with a customs officer.

'Well,' Anna observed, 'things seem to be fairly normal here.'

'Normal chaos,' James agreed. 'But no army in sight. We're in luck. These people will have no reason to stop us. We'll have no trouble, I'm certain. We'll just wait quietly and remain inconspicuous and when it's our turn we'll do everything they say, hand over the dollars and we'll be through.'

'Right,' said Anna, beginning to feel herself relax a little for the first time in twenty-four hours. She looked out of the window and nodded contentedly to herself. Kidaho felt as it should. Like the old Rwanda, the Africa she knew. The smell of banana beer wafted from one of the huts and the air was heavy with the sweet scent of strong African tobacco. One or two local people were setting up their wares for sale. A woman spread a colourful rush mat on the ground, then laid out neatly upon it a dozen hard, green mangoes and a large handful of salt for their buyers to dip them in. An old, wizened man, smoking a clay pipe, sat with his back against the wall of one of the buildings. The little store had hanging from its porch rafters one of the most recognizable icons in the world, *Coca Cola*. It was reassuring in its familiarity, proving somehow that in spite of war, in spite of terrible events, the world outside, was still there.

'We'll head straight for the British Embassy in Kampala when we're through,' James said. 'They'll be able to ring Nairobi and find out about Mum and Dad and let them know we're safe.'

'I can't wait to see them,' Anna said.

She turned her head as some soft footsteps approached from behind the vehicle and the delicious smell of newly baked bread drifted into their nostrils.

Alfred growled appreciatively and expectantly as a tall woman in a brightly coloured wrap-around *kanga* swayed elegantly past them with a huge basket of bread on her head.

'Oh,' said Anna. 'Quick. James, pass me a few francs and I'll get some of that. I'm starving.'

'So am I,' said James. He burrowed in his pocket and passed her some money.

Anna climbed out of the Range Rover and followed the woman. She caught up with her near the front of the queue. Just ahead of them the barrier was suddenly lifted and the Asian businessman waved through. There was a brief burst of activity as all the other vehicles in the line started up their engines and lurched forward one place. Then it became quiet again as the engines were switched off and their owners settled down for the next wait.

Or almost quiet.

As Anna began to haggle with the bread-seller she became conscious of a low rumble, as of distant thunder. She looked up at the sky. It was blue and cloudless. Then she looked up at the mountains. They too were clear and still and quiet. She put her head

41

slightly on one side and listened carefully. The roar was getting louder by the second. She lifted her head and looked south-east towards Kigali.

Briefly her heart leapt. But that was before she had had time to think. For one happy moment she thought that the helicopters streaming, *pouring* in towards them, were United Nations helicopters coming back for them.

But that, of course, was nonsense. The UN soldiers had gone and would not come back.

As she watched, one of the approaching helicopters detached itself from the rest. It slowed, sank down and hovered just above the ground. Two armed soldiers jumped out, ducked down and moved away from it. They waited briefly until it rose again, then they walked away from each other. Another helicopter leapfrogged the first and repeated the manoeuvre. The men it disgorged took up positions close to where they were dropped.

Anna handed her money to the bread-seller. The woman pressed a large, warm loaf under each of Anna's arms. 'Thank you,' Anna whispered. Then she turned and began to walk back to the Range Rover.

The Asian businessman's pick-up raised a cloud of dust as it set off down the road to Cyanika. No doubt he was unaware of his good fortune, unaware that he would be the last person to leave Rwanda for days. Or weeks.

The heavy steel barrier clanged down behind him. Probably none of the people hearing it realized the finality of that clang at that moment.

But Anna did.

She climbed sadly back into the Range Rover. The

roar of the helicopters increased as they powered westwards and the clang of the barrier echoed in her head.

'The rebel army's here,' she said. 'They're dropping soldiers all along the border. They're sealing it, along all its length. There's no way out.'

James started the engine and reversed the Range Rover rapidly down the road. Then he spun it round and headed away from the border post, back towards Ruhengeri.

'What now?' he asked, despondently.

No one could think of an answer.

Behind them a giant Sikorski helicopter sank down on to the ground in no man's land. The cargo hatch at the back crashed open, raising a cloud of red dust which was whisked into a small tornado by the screaming rotors. From out of the dust, one by one, four jeeps emerged, each filled with grim-faced Tutsi soldiers holding machine-guns in their hands.

The government hostel in Ruhengeri was the ideal place to hide for a while. It was surrounded by a dense, high hedge. Once it would have been full. So full that extra beds would have been hauled into its dormitories and out into its gardens to accommodate the huge numbers of backpackers who swarmed through Africa.

The war had stopped all that, of course. For months only the hardiest, or foolhardiest, tourists had braved Rwanda. Probably the only guests here in the last six months had been foreign journalists desperately seeking ever more lurid stories of tribal feuds and bloodshed and cannibalism to shock their readers back home.

Today the large, rambling hostel was silent and deserted. The garden was empty and overgrown.

'Pull the Range Rover round the back,' Anna suggested. 'Just in case anyone sees it from the road.'

James negotiated it round the building and tucked it in close to a shed. They climbed out and walked back round to the front door. It stood open. Its glass was smashed.

'Wait here,' Dominic said. 'There is someone I know close by. I will try to get help. I will return soon.' He padded across the grass and vanished through the hedge.

They watched him go, then went up the steps.

'What do you think?' Anna asked. 'Do you trust him?'

'I don't know. He seems to be all right. Although there don't seem to me to be any "goodies" in this war, just "baddies". There seems to be no honour. No rules. No "just causes". Anyway, it's not up to us to judge. It's not our fight, we're just in the crossfire. If he comes back, he comes back. If he doesn't we fend for ourselves.'

'Can we fend for ourselves?' Anna asked. 'To be honest, I'm frightened out of my mind.'

'I know. So am I. But that won't help us.'

'We can catch our breath here anyway,' Anna suggested, as she and James entered the building. 'While we try and figure out what to do.'

They found themselves in a large untidy room. A few mismatched tables and some dilapidated wicker chairs were strewn around. At the end of the room a large, louvred window looked out on to the garden.

They pulled two chairs up to a glass-topped table. A solitary cockroach broke off from feeding on the remains of some long-abandoned meal and waved its feelers in perfunctory enquiry. James kicked the table leg. The cockroach scuttled across the glass, dropped down to the floor with a stomach-turning, hollow *clack* and disappeared through a gap in the floorboards. *Where, no doubt*, James thought silently, *it has joined a million others*. The thought of the seething mass of them that probably boiled, like living soup, centimetres below their feet made him feel sick.

'I don't suppose we're safe here,' Anna said. 'People will have seen us drive in.'

'We'll have to risk it for a while. We need to eat something. And we need to get these cuts cleaned up or they'll be septic before we know it. Then we'll have a council of war – if that's not too unfortunate a way of putting it.'

'Right,' said Anna. 'I'll find the washrooms. Although I don't suppose there'll be any soap, or any plugs in the basins, or any towels.' She set off down a long corridor, her voice becoming fainter as she progressed. 'Or even, as this is Rwanda,' she added, trying a door-handle, 'any water.'

'How do you feel now?' James asked.

They had made some jam sandwiches in the hostel's deserted kitchens and brewed some strong tea. Anna had a plaster over her eye and James had bound his skinned shins with bandages made from strips of bedsheet.

45

'Terrified. Daunted. Worried to death about what Mum and Dad are going through. Homesick.' Anna smiled ruefully. 'But apart from that, all right. All in all we didn't come out of the crash too badly. My head hurts a bit from the knock it took, but it's bearable. How are your legs?'

'They'll be all right so long as I keep them covered to stop them getting infected.'

They were silent for a moment.

'What are we going to do?' Anna looked round disconsolately.

'I don't know. We shouldn't hang around here for too long. My guess is the rebel army will roll in and start to clear the town soon, so they can loot it. By nightfall Ruhengeri will be on fire, like Kigali was last night. The soldiers will be out of control, filling trucks with whatever they can lay their hands on. And it won't matter whether you're Tutsi or Hutu or Asian, black or white, male, female, young or old. If you're in the way, you'll be trampled.'

'It's all looking a bit hopeless, isn't it?' Anna stared out at the garden. 'I wish Mum and Dad were here. Dad would come up with something.'

'I think this situation might even have been beyond his ingenuity. I can't think where we can hide, and with the borders closed it's impossible to escape. So, without a miracle, we're in very deep trouble.'

'I don't believe in miracles,' Anna said.

They sat in silence.

Eventually Anna got up. She wandered over to the reception desk, idly picked up the telephone and listened. It was no surprise to find that it was not working. To the side of the desk was a rack of colourful leaflets advertising the wonders of Rwanda. Now dog-eared, chewed by cockroaches and sagging with damp, they were a stark reminder of the days when tourists thronged the country, their current decay a powerful symbol of what Rwanda had become. She picked one from the rack. On the front was a smiling, radiantly healthy Rwandan woman of great beauty, with scarlet hibiscus flowers in her hair.

VISIT RWANDA – JEWEL OF AFRICA

ordered the *Office Rwandais du Tourisme et des Parcs Nationaux*.

She snorted derisively. 'If you want to get arrested or shot,' she said to herself.

Another leaflet featured a picture of the perfect, soaring volcanic cone of Mount Karisimbi.

PARC NATIONAL DES VOLCANS

She picked it up and idly glanced through it. The volcanoes were listed, each with brief details of how to ascend them.

A popular climb is to the top of Mount Visoke volcano (3,711 metres). The climb takes approximately seven hours, culminating in one of the most beautiful crater lakes in Africa. Visoke means 'The Place Where Cattle Are Watered'.

For the more ambitious there is Mount Karisimbi (4,507 metres) the ascent of which will take two days. The name comes from *nsimbi*, white cowry shells; the cone of the volcano is often covered with hail and resembles the shells. Guides and porters are recommended for this ascent!

To the north-east is Mount Sabinio (named 'Father of the Teeth' – because of its tooth-like ridges) (3,634 metres). This climb takes six hours. At the summit three countries – Rwanda, Uganda and The Democratic Republic of Congo – join.

And further north-east still are Mount Gahinga ('The Cultivated Hill') (3,474 metres) and Mount Muhavura ('He Who Shows The Way') (4,127 metres), about two-thirds of which are in Rwanda, the other third being in Uganda.

'What have you got there?' James asked.

'Just an old leaflet,' Anna replied, throwing it down. She returned to the table and sat down beside James. 'About climbing the volcanoes.'

They sat morosely staring into space for long minutes. Outside, the heavy drum of diesel engines in the distance signalled the arrival of the Tutsi army.

Suddenly Anna leaped to her feet, crossed the room and picked up the leaflet again.

The words *about two-thirds of which are in Rwanda, the other third being in Uganda* jumped off the page.

'James,' she said. 'I wouldn't go so far as to call this a miracle, but I wouldn't think it very likely they'll be putting border guards on the tops of mountains.'

James looked up. 'What?'

'The mountains. The Virungas. They all have borders with other countries. We could walk over them. Get down the other side of Sabinio into the Congo say, or Muhavura into Uganda.'

James grinned. 'Brilliant,' he said. 'Absolutely brilliant.'

Anna handed the leaflet to him.

'Muhavura I think,' he said. 'The Congo is in

turmoil too. As it always is. They might just send us straight back again.'

There was a noise from outside.

'Shush.' Anna signalled urgently. 'There's someone coming.'

They looked anxiously out of the window. Two figures in camouflage uniform had entered the garden. They were standing close to the gate casually lighting cigarettes.

James drew in his breath sharply. Rebel soldiers.

Anna backed silently away from the door into the room. She peered through the louvred window and shook her head in dismay. Neither of the 'soldiers' could have been more than thirteen years old. Boys in men's uniforms, with AK-47s slung over their shoulders. These were the most dangerous, the most feared of all. The child killers trained by the Tutsi army to shoot without discretion. Without asking why or who.

They began to stroll casually down the drive towards the hostel. There was nothing boyish about their bearing. They walked with the strange rolling gait that they cultivated and practised. A swagger that spoke of their complete confidence in themselves and in the gun.

Alfred, lying under the table, began to growl. Anna immediately whispered to him and took a step towards him to silence him. She was too late. The growl turned into a loud snarl and he jumped up to his feet, knocking the glass top off the table. It fell to the floor and shattered with a heart-stopping crash.

The soldiers paused briefly. Then, with a speed and

49

smoothness that spoke of long practice, their guns were off their shoulders and in their hands.

'Oh no,' James whispered. Slowly he and Anna started to back across the room. Alfred hurtled towards the door, snarling furiously.

'Quick,' Anna said.

They spun round and ran down the corridor towards the kitchens and the back door. As they ran, a burst of gunfire rattled out behind them. There was a sound of splintering wood. They heard Alfred yelp. His snarling stopped.

Then they were out of the building and running hard towards the concealed Range Rover. Anna called out to Alfred as she ran. But he did not come.

More gunfire. The crash of breaking glass.

They flung open the doors of the Range Rover and scrambled in. Panic made James's hand tremble violently as he tried to put the key into the ignition.

'Quickly,' Anna pleaded. She called Alfred's name one more time.

James fumbled more and dropped the key. He gasped at his clumsiness, then scrabbled frantically in the footwell. The soldiers emerged from the back door and began to descend the steps.

'James,' Anna cried. 'Quickly. They're coming.'

James regained the key, took a deep breath to steady himself and found the ignition. He turned the key. The engine fired immediately. He slammed the gears into reverse and shot backwards towards the hedge. Fear made him misjudge the distance and he braked too late. The back of the vehicle slammed into the hedge and the glass tailgate shattered.

He spun the steering wheel, engaged second gear

and put his foot down hard. The vehicle hesitated momentarily, its wheels spinning on the grass, then the tyres bit and it powered across the garden towards the main gate. Just as the two soldiers rounded the corner.

Instinctively James lifted his foot off the accelerator. But only for a split second. Logic quickly returned as the soldiers' guns swung towards them. He slammed his foot down again and drove straight at them.

Briefly he saw uncertainty flash across the soldiers' faces as the vehicle roared towards them. Then they both tried to jump out of the way.

Only one made it.

There was a dull thud. Anna gasped with shock as the soldier crashed to the ground in front of them.

James braked hard and the vehicle skidded into the hedge. Anna spun round in her seat and looked behind. The other soldier was scrambling to his feet. His gun lay on the grass several metres away from him. In the space of a split second he located it with his eyes and began to run towards it.

James reversed and spun the steering wheel again.

The other soldier was almost on his gun. He bent down as he approached it, ready to sweep it up as he ran.

'Hurry, James,' Anna gasped. 'If he gets his gun we're finished.'

As she said it, she became aware of another figure emerging from round the side of the building, a tall figure, bare-chested and barefoot, wearing only a pair of ragged blue shorts. He was running at full speed, heading directly for the soldier. Or rather for the gun, because he launched himself into a headlong dive, grasped the AK-47 and rolled skilfully out of the soldier's way. As he came up out of the roll on to his knees he was levelling the gun at the soldier.

The rebel soldier stopped in his tracks. He looked momentarily at the gun, then fear spread across his face and he turned and fled.

It was a moment before Anna and James recognized their saviour. He had shaved his head and he was covered with red dust.

'There,' he said, as he approached. 'I look a bit less like a president's son now, eh?'

Anna turned and headed back to the hostel. She called out Alfred's name a final time, but knew in her heart that it was no good.

She found him just inside the doorway.

'Oh no,' she gasped, as she dropped to her knees beside him.

Tears filled her eyes.

'My poor boy,' she whispered, as she stroked his lifeless head.

'Your plan is possible, but very dangerous,' Dominic pronounced. He was sitting in the front of the Range Rover with James, tuning the radio as they left town. 'My friend was too frightened to help. He told me to listen to what the Tutsi are broadcasting and I'd see why.'

The radio crackled and then a voice broke out; the soft, measured voice of Colonel Ruvenga Kanyaragana, the new Head of State, speaking from Kigali.

My people, he began, *our ordeal is nearly at an end.*

A quietly spoken sentence. But a million Hutu

shuddered and began to wonder where they could hide. For 'my people' meant simply 'my tribe'. The WaTutsi.

It has been a long ordeal, he continued. *But now our enemies are on the run. Yesterday the lap-dog soldiers of the western colonialist oppressors fled. The puppet President Seregera is dead and his criminal family will be arrested, as will any who harbour or aid them. The disgraced BaHutu Government of this country is no more. Now your People's Army is in charge. Now the wheel has turned. In the Congo and Burundi, in Uganda and Tanzania and Kenya, exiled WaTutsi will be turning their eyes and their feet towards their homeland. Those driven out by colonial oppressors, white and black, will now return.*

'So, there you have it,' said James to Dominic. 'We're "colonial oppressors", you're "a criminal" and we're "harbouring and aiding" you.'

'Yes,' said Dominic. 'For the moment.'

'Heaven help us all then,' Anna whispered. 'Especially your tribe.'

Dominic nodded.

'We are all in great danger now,' he said. He stared thoughtfully out of the window at the passing landscape. 'And I have made your danger greater by being with you. I am sorry.'

'No,' James said. 'Things were out of control anyway.'

Kanyaragana's voice was beginning to rise.

They return to take possession of what is theirs, what was stolen from them. Now is the time of reckoning. Now is the time for the WaTutsi to rise and reclaim this beautiful land of Rwanda. Those of you

53

who have taken what is not yours will now give it back. Those of you who have persecuted will now receive retribution. The destroyers will now be destroyed.

'Switch it off, James,' Anna pleaded. 'I can't stand to hear it.'

James clicked the switch. They sat in silence, dismayed by what they had heard.

'Even if you make it to the mountain, your plan is still too dangerous,' said Dominic eventually.

'Why?' James asked.

'Because not only do many Tutsi live in the forest, it is also full of animals. The buffalo there are dangerous and unpredictable and there are gorillas which have been known to tear men apart. A fully grown male gorilla can weigh up to two hundred kilograms and he will kill to protect his group. You are already in grave danger because you have helped me. If the animals don't get you, the Tutsi will. I found my friend and his family cowering in fear. Hutu everywhere are cowering in fear. It is not right for me to run away. But I will help you get away if I can.'

'How?' Anna asked.

'I know a place, a Hutu village where we may get help.'

They turned a corner. The tarmac road petered out and turned into dirt. James put his foot down. The compass on the dashboard showed west and the road stretched as far as the eye could see. Far in the distance the soaring volcanoes of the Virungas reared up through low cloud, their white peaks floating on cotton wool.

*

54

An hour later they drove into Kinigi village.

They were not surprised to find that it had the appearance at first of being deserted. The broadcast had made the approach of any vehicle a thing to be feared.

As the Range Rover drove slowly through the dilapidated collection of houses, past tiny stores which once had sold souvenirs to the tourists, the occupants of the village kept themselves hidden. Here a ragged curtain would twitch, there a shadow would melt into a deeper shadow.

'Eerie,' said Anna.

'It's going to get worse before it gets better.' James peered sadly at the houses.

'Kanyaragana's speech was an open invitation to massacre my people,' Dominic said. 'And they will seek out any who have helped my people and punish them too.'

Neither James nor Anna answered him. The age-old conflict was a circle. Last time the Hutu, Dominic's people, had massacred the Tutsi. *The wheel has turned*, Kanyaragana said. In Rwanda the wheel revolved every generation.

'We're coming up to a crossroad.' James slowed the vehicle down.

Parc Headquarters 2kms Gasiza 20kms a sign announced.

'There,' Dominic said. 'Gasiza. It is the Hutu village where my father's family came from. There we should be able to get help.'

James swung the Range Rover right.

Remnants of better times began to emerge at the roadsides. Abandoned, overturned stalls where once vegetables and fresh eggs and pressed lemonade could have been bought. A board, barely legible now, offering bicycles and tents for hire spoke eloquently of a normal life now lost. Finally a large peeling sign announced:

Parc National des Volcans

They drove through the entrance and pulled up outside the main building. It was deserted and derelict. The front doors had been wrenched completely off.

'I remember this,' Anna said. 'We came here when I was small.'

James switched the engine off and they all got out and looked around. The clouds had cleared a little to the south-west and Visoke was emerging through curtains of rain. The greater bulk of Karisimbi was still obscured, but its pure white cone was visible high above the clouds. Dominic went up the steps into the building. They followed him into what had been the reception area. It was hard to imagine the noise and excitement it would once have housed as tourists clamoured to have their permits checked and fought for tickets for transport to the climbing routes or wildlife viewing areas. Now it was just a bare room, anything removable having long ago been stolen.

The floor was littered with papers and leaflets. Dominic dropped on to his haunches and started sifting through them.

'What are you looking for?' Anna asked.

'Maps,' Dominic answered. 'There are huts on the mountains where climbers used to stay. My father's government built them and many tourists came to Rwanda because of them. Now they are unused. I

56

think it best you drop me off near Gasiza village so you are not seen. The fewer people who know you are here the better. For your sake and theirs. It will be safer if you go to the mountains and wait until I have organized some help. You should not cross into the Impenetrable Forest without some protection. I will come to you when I know more about how things are.'

He picked up a printed map and handed it to James.

'Here. Muhavura.'

Anna and James studied the map. It clearly showed the route of ascent for Mount Muhavura and the positions of the climbers' huts.

'The first hut looks about 300 metres up into the forest,' James observed, studying the map carefully.

'And if that turns out to be no good there's a second hut further up,' Anna added.

James folded the map and stuffed it into his shirt pocket.

'I will find you,' Dominic said. 'Now, let us go on.'

James noticed that Anna looked dejected. 'Cheer up,' he said. 'Things will be all right.'

'I believe you,' said Anna. She stared at the distant mountains. Dark clouds were gathering ominously around them. 'There's not much choice but to be optimistic, is there?'

Nine

Waa-urgh. Waa-urgh. Waa-Urgh.

He rolled from his nest and was on his feet straight away. A bolt of fear passed through him, instinct preparing him, flooding adrenaline through his blood.

The group was in great agitation. The childless females were huddled together screaming and hooting with anxiety, whilst those with newborn infants clinging to them hid fearfully behind. The young blackback males were chest-beating, dancing out into the forest in mock forays of attack and crashing immediately back again to the sleeping site. The terrified older infants had ascended into trees, each as high as their climbing skill would take them, where they clung desperately to swaying branches, or each other, and screamed with panic.

The noise was cataclysmic. It drilled into his head, numbing his sleep-befuddled mind.

Loping rapidly across the clearing he cuffed a couple of the young males, sending them spinning head over heels into the bush. Then he came to a halt, reared himself upright on his legs, battered his chest in rapid staccato with his clenched fists and bellowed for silence.

The chatters and grunts and screechings died away. The group shuffled into stillness and waited expectantly.

He leaned forward, knuckles thudding into the soft earth, furrowed his leathery brow with concentration and listened hard.

A confusion of sounds. The yapping of dogs and the clanging of the bells round their necks. The bells which would tell the men where they were and bring them running. And a long, pain-charged moaning, deep at first, from the pit of the stomach, but rising, becoming a scream and tailing off into a chatter of terror.

A voice he knew. One of his own group. One of the females. Crying out in distress. Trapped. Harried.

He snarled with rage, turning his head from side to side, identifying, *sifting* the sounds, listening for the men.

If there were dogs there were men. Where were they? Nothing else mattered. Nothing anywhere in the forest mattered, nothing posed a danger as great as men.

He could hear them. Shouting. Well away from the dogs.

He was on the move almost before the conscious decision filtered into his brain. All the experience his age had brought him, all the strength built over long years, all his hard-won cunning and bravery, were to one end only.

To protect.

Oblivious now of anything except the cries of distress, he pounded across the clearing and crashed into the bush. Head down, he punched through the hanging mats of vines and tangled saplings, his great weight smashing the dense vegetation aside as though it did not exist.

Ahead of his pounding descent snakes hissed hurriedly out of danger, raising rainbow clouds of butterflies into the air; bright birds screeched in alarm and batted higher up into the trees, where startled monkeys dislodged themselves in hysterical, whooping leaps from branch to branch; the silent leopard woke from almost-sleep and wafted away on feet of air: even the great, grey buffalo, immovable, solid as stones, afraid of nothing, took a passing interest and raised their massively horned heads and snuffled irritably.

Behind him, taking his lead, following the well-rehearsed order of things, the defensive convoy assembled in military hierarchy. The other silverbacks, younger than he but experienced and capable, sometimes a challenge to his authority but now, in time of threat, supporting him, roared down the path at his heels. On their heels the blackbacks, eager but undisciplined, flailed along in disarray, trying to appear brave but chattering with nerves. Bringing up the rear, the camp-followers, the juveniles with little idea of what was going on and the anxious females, fearful for everyone, screeched with excitement and terror. For all the world a medieval, *tribal*, battle encounter. An attack on an individual bringing the whole village whooping out in defence.

He knew they were pouring down the mountainside behind him, following the flag of his great silver back through the gloom of the forest. Following their leader, the one who knew what to do.

The dogs, swarming like huge ants over the terrified female, probably didn't even hear the great bellow of fury he gave out as he smashed into the clearing.

Certainly some did not live long enough even to begin to comprehend what was happening. Perhaps a great, dark shadow looming above them briefly entered their consciousness in their last seconds.

The first two died instantly as he grasped them by their necks and picked them off their prey. Their spines snapped like twigs in his great hands, their heads lolled and their tongues rolled out of their mouths. They were big dogs, heavy with muscle built from years of fighting and eating good meat, but they sailed through the air as though weightless, their bells ringing their death-knell now as he tossed them disdainfully away.

He selected two more and repeated the action. And by then was joined by the other silverbacks.

The blackbacks and the females gathered around the edges of the clearing, remaining in the protection of the trees but urging the combatants on with whoops and bellows of encouragement.

The younger silverbacks had begun to attack now, lashing out at the snapping pack with great flailing fists, knocking dogs off the now tentatively retaliating female. Snarls turned to howls as the broken-backed squirmed in agony on the ground, vainly trying to rise and run again.

And then the moment of surprise passed. Realizing what was happening, the remains of the pack suddenly hurled themselves off the female, exploded away from her like shrapnel from a bomb and turned to face their attackers.

Immediately the terrified and weakened female staggered shakily to her feet, paused uncertainly for a second or two as though unable to believe her miraculous release, then scuttled across the clearing. The group accepted her back with cries of greeting and recognition. A great hooting and chattering went up from females, blackbacks and infants alike. Briefly they all surrounded her, inspecting her, then tucking her safely in the centre of the group, began to pour back up the mountainside again. Their nerves, stretched like piano-wire by the events, now found release from tension in a deafening chorus of raucous screeches and whoops and howls of pure triumph.

And in the clearing, as the sound of the departing group lessened, became muffled by deadening forest and distance, the clean-up continued.

Poachers' dogs are not bred to accept defeat. They do not run away. But nor do silverback gorillas defending their own. For them there is no concept of retreat or compromise.

For both, every fight is to the death.

Mouths slavering with ferocity, bloodied fangs glinting, eyes rolling white with rage, the pack encircled the four silverbacks, then slowly began to close in on them.

Back to back, knotted together in tight unity, standing tall, the silverbacks opened their mouths and roared in defiance, their great canine jaws spreading wide to reveal terrible fangs of their own. Then they hammered their chests briefly and without more ado engaged battle.

The scene became a maelstrom of whirling bodies, sharply snapping jaws, flailing arms and legs, a pandemonium of shrieks and snarls.

It was an uneven battle.

There was in the end only one outcome.

The dogs inflicted damage. They were big and powerful and determined. They hurled themselves at the gorillas' legs and arms and bodies and throats. Their jaws locked on and sank in, deep in muscle, deep sometimes to the bone. But few things are a match for a silverback gorilla, a creature of awesome power.

One by one, the dogs were smashed into the ground by great pounding fists, their skulls crushed like eggshells, or plucked disdainfully off a great hairy leg or arm and thrown against a tree, to lie broken and dying. Or they were simply picked up in a hand so massive and powerful that a single squeeze of the fingers was enough to snap a neck.

It was all over in minutes. In repetitive pattern. A snarl of attack which would transmute into a howl of pain, into a whimper, into silence.

Again and again and again, until there was no sound in the blood-stained, body-littered clearing but the laboured breathing of the four silverbacks as they stood surveying their triumph.

Then they began to withdraw. The three junior silverbacks turned, dropped their knuckles to the earth and slowly – swaying and strutting and swinging their heads in display of contemptuous nonchalance – they walked into the bush and began to make their way after the rest of the group.

Leaving their leader to have the final word.

He stood still for a minute.

His great, barrel chest heaved rapidly as he gasped air into his lungs. Vaguely, he was aware of pains here and there. But mostly the pains were slight. Except for one. He looked curiously at his hand. It was badly bitten. He put it to his mouth and licked away the blood. Then he shook it to see if the pain went away. It didn't. He turned his attention away from it.

He listened carefully now. The heat of the battle had consumed all thought, all attention. But all the time, in the back of his mind, was the most important danger.

The men.

Where were they?

He shut his eyes the better to hear, the clearer to position them. And found them, a long way down the mountainside. Creeping softly through the forest. Too far away to be an immediate danger.

He rose high up on his legs, raised the comb of hair on the top of his head into full display to magnify his size, and took a deep breath to increase the drum-resonance of his lung cavity.

Then, with the defiant, contemptuous leisure of the triumphant, he beat his chest.

POK . . . POK . . . POK.

The rustlings below faded away.

Then came the final word.

He raised his arms high, opened his great mouth and bellowed down the mountainside.

WAAAAAAAARHG-HUH!

Half an hour later a band of sweating men walked into the clearing.

Barefoot, with bare legs emerging from shorts deliberately cut ragged, they were dressed mainly in tattered remnants of European clothes, discards of expatriates long gone or lootings from aid packages. There was an old army greatcoat here, a sweatshirt with NEW YORK NEW YORK printed on it there; a white evening-dress shirt with frills down the front but the sleeves torn out here, an old houndstooth sports jacket there. Baseball caps and mirror-sunglasses were evenly distributed throughout the group, as were large, ostentatious watches, most of which didn't work, which didn't matter as their wearers weren't able to tell the time.

A strange collection of humanity, dressed in the sinister, mocking apparel of the fashion-conscious African killer.

In their hands were machetes and bows and arrows. One carried an ancient elephant gun. Another an automatic rifle.

They surveyed, with incredulity, the destruction of their most prized possession, their single most valuable asset.

At first they were speechless.

Their hunting pack gone!

When they began to talk again quietly amongst themselves it would not have mattered whether you understood their language, Kinyarwanda, or not. It would not have mattered if, like the animals, you understood no language at all.

What they were saying, as they stared up the mountain, was quite obvious.

For their words hissed, *boiled*, with vengeance.

Ten

The rain clouds were gathering on the mountains as they ground up the slopes from Gasiza village.

The barren, hail-scoured summit of Mount Muhavura was just disappearing from view, but Mount Gahinga, 600 metres lower, was still completely visible.

Sun played on the long, high-meadow strip which joined the two mountains, though the clouds were threatening to roll down and obscure that too.

'How's the petrol?' Anna asked.

'Not good. The low-fuel light came on a few kilometres back. I was hoping we'd get well up towards the saddle between the two mountains, but I think that's a bit optimistic now.'

'Aim for Gahinga's lower slopes then. If there's still petrol left when we get there, we'll skirt round the base a bit and see how high we can get up before we have to walk.'

The slopes they were traversing were cultivated, but only sparsely inhabited. Where possible, James had tried to keep clear of any habitation at all, but here and there they passed the occasional hut from which frightened faces would peer out at them. No one was working in the *shambas*. Those with portable radios would have heard the colonel's broadcast, those without would quickly have been told. Work had ceased. Cattle wandered untended.

'Pity we're so visible,' said James.

Anna shook her head. 'I don't think it matters. These people will all be too busy with their own affairs now to be concerned about us. Another kilometre and we'll be away from open country and into the tree line anyway. Once the Range Rover's hidden in the trees we won't be spotted even from the air.'

James pulled the map from his shirt pocket and handed it to Anna.

'Have a look and see if you can identify just where the climber's track begins,' he said.

She studied the map. 'About the centre of the mountain really,' she said.

James adjusted the line the Range Rover was taking and pointed it to the centre of Muhavura's bulk. The clouds were sweeping down the mountain now, the deep green of the forest painted with long smoke-skeins of grey, rain-laden and ominous.

'Looks a bit fearful up there,' Anna observed.

'Yes. But the hut shouldn't take too long to reach. Three hundred metres isn't far.'

The cultivated slopes abutted directly on to the forest at about 3,000 metres. James stopped as they approached the tree line.

'We made it,' James said, patting the Range Rover affectionately on the dashboard. 'The old girl always makes it. Now we'll see if we can find the entrance to the track. According to the map we should be quite close.' He engaged gear again and drove slowly along, parallel to the trees. Many of the *shambas* here had fallen into disuse and showed signs of being trampled by forest animals. Some were destroyed completely and droppings showed unmistakable evidence of elephants.

'I thought elephants were all gone from here,' Anna said. 'Some have obviously survived. They've made a mess of that bean patch.'

'Hmm. Let's hope we don't meet them. That's all we need, to get charged by a bull elephant.'

The engine of the Range Rover coughed. The vehicle lurched, then recovered its even note.

'Uh-oh,' said Anna.

A few metres farther on it coughed again and died. The petrol pump ticked rapidly. The tank was empty.

They climbed out.

'Right,' James said. 'The sooner we're in the forest the better. Let's get collected up. Essentials only, I think.'

He walked round to the back of the vehicle.

'A change of clothes each would be a good idea,' Anna advised. 'We might get a bit wet later this afternoon by the look of things.'

'Yes.' James began to rummage through the bags. 'And warm coats or sweaters each. It gets very cold up here at night.'

'And the rice and biscuits you stole,' Anna reminded him. 'I'll carry those if you like.' She opened her bag and began to empty it of all the treasures she had packed to take to Nairobi, tossing them on to the back seat.

She glanced briefly at each.

'Funny,' she said. 'When I was packing I thought I couldn't do without any of these. Now they don't seem to matter at all. I thought they were memories. But they're not. They're only things. Memories are in your head.'

'Nothing like being in danger of your life to put things in perspective, is there?' asked James.

He pulled his climbing boots out of his bag and started to put them on.

'Aren't you glad now I persuaded you to pack your boots?'

'I am, yes.'

Anna noticed the machete wedged behind the seat.

'It might be useful to take this,' she said, reaching in for it.

'Good thinking,' James agreed. 'And my climbing rope and head-torch.'

He draped the coiled rope over his shoulder.

'And now there's just one thing left to do,' he announced. He placed his rucksack on the ground. 'If you'd just like to step away from the Range Rover,' he said.

Then he leaned in through the driver's door, knocked the gear lever into neutral and released the handbrake. The vehicle creaked ominously and began to move. James slammed the door and stepped out of the way.

'It's called "destroying the evidence". Gangsters always do it in films, push their getaway cars down hills or over cliffs.'

The Range Rover was gathering speed down the slope, creaking and groaning as it bounced over tussocks of grass.

'And,' he added, warming to his subject, 'they

always do very spectacular airborne acrobatics, finally exploding in huge fireballs.'

'I think you'd need petrol for that, wouldn't you?'

'Spoilsport,' said James. 'Come on, let's go. It'll end up down at the base of the mountain, hopefully in some trees. But if anyone finds it right down there it won't matter. We'll be long gone. If we'd left it here they'd know we were in the forest.'

The Range Rover had disappeared from sight. They turned away and began to ascend the slope. There was a muffled bang from far below.

'Fifteen years we had that car,' said Anna. 'All my life.'

'Hmm,' said James glumly, 'it's probably just run over someone's cow. So we'll have them chasing us, as well as the rebel army.'

'Dominic will smooth things out for us. I hope he can get help.'

'So do I. The quicker the better. Though if we find somewhere safe we'll wait a few days. If no help comes we'll just have to risk going over the top into Uganda by ourselves.'

'How much longer before we admit we can't find it?'

James looked at his watch. 'Five minutes. We'll have been walking exactly two hours then.'

They had skirted along the line of the forest. Up close it was forbidding in its density. It was like following a towering green wall.

'It's overgrown, obviously,' Anna concluded. 'And if the entrance is overgrown then the track itself will be. We might as well cut our losses and just start to climb anywhere.'

70

'An overgrown track is better than no track,' James insisted. 'If we try to fight our own way up it will be tremendously difficult. You can see how dense it is. And on top of that, if we don't find the track we don't stand much chance of finding the hut.'

Ahead of them a startled bush pig ran out of the forest into the open, squealed with alarm and ran back again.

'He knows his way in,' Anna observed.

'He's half our size and twice as nimble,' James replied.

They explored the spot where the pig had vanished. James followed the broken vegetation of its panicked flight into the forest for a couple of metres and found himself at the entrance to a tunnel.

'This might be it,' he called. 'Come and have a look.'

The entrance was overgrown. He pushed aside the tangle of vines and peered in. The tunnel was about two metres wide and a soft, green light at the far end showed that it was about twenty metres long. A cool, dim lava corridor leading into the forest.

'This looks very promising,' Anna remarked.

James stepped inside. The walls and roof had crumbled over the years and his feet sank into a deep layer of gravelly dust. He looked down. There were numerous animal footprints.

'A track,' he announced.

They made their way cautiously through and found themselves magically transported into another world.

No entrance could have been more dramatic. Twenty metres in and a curtain had been drawn upon the outside world.

They emerged on to dimly lit, densely vegetated slopes angling steeply upwards. A track of sorts was visible, but only just; a narrow pathway rather than a track, discernible only because the vegetation was lower. Huge *Hagenia* trees reared high above their heads forming a dense canopy through which soft light filtered and broke, as through a prism. Massive in girth and almost totally covered with mosses and lichens, the *Hagenias* had purple flowers that glowed against a patchwork of greens of every shade. Brilliant emerald narrowleaf ferns hung in cascades from their branches, each a bright fountain spurting from a bed of moss. Luminous orchids spattered the trees with colour like Christmas lights and long hangings of vines swooped dramatically and untidily from invisible heights down to the ground.

Between the *Hagenias* tall *Hypericum* trees fought for space. Almost as tall as their neighbours, they looked spindly and frail beside them. Too weak to bear the heavy mosses, they still could not escape some burden. Between their tiny leaves and yellow flowers, wisps of lichen tumbled like strands of untameable hair and the red-flowered mistletoe *Loranthus* clustered in bunches at the bases of all their branches.

Squeezed tightly into small clumps, *Veronia* claimed what space they could. Half the height of the other trees, their white-petalled, lavender-tipped flowers were bright will-o'-the-wisps flashing in the subdued light.

It was cool and wet and almost silent. The only sound was a gentle wind softly stirring the high branches. The forest exuded vast age and complete peace. Twenty metres behind them humanity, with its petty squabbles and greeds, had been stopped, the door closed against it.

Slowly their eyes adjusted to the soft light.

'So beautiful,' Anna whispered. 'I don't think I've ever seen anything so beautiful.' She stared up into the canopy high above them. 'I feel as though I'm in a cathedral. Ancient and cool.'

'The map doesn't show a tunnel,' James mused. 'That's a bit strange. You'd have thought an unusual feature like that would be the obvious thing to mention.'

'You don't think this is the right one then?'

'I don't know. I'm just puzzled.'

'Well, it's a track,' Anna said. 'And it goes upwards. That's all that matters, isn't it? Sometimes you make difficulties where there aren't any. Let's get on our way.'

Difficulties soon began.

The path was very steep and very slippy. Moss-covered rocks lurked just below ground-cover vegetation, lying in wait for unsuspecting feet to slide off them.

But what they had most seriously underestimated was the altitude. They were starting their climb at over three thousand metres.

At three thousand metres the air becomes very thin.

Soon they were gasping for breath, their lungs rasping with the effort of obtaining oxygen and their hearts pumping with frightening resonance in their ears.

'I can't go another step,' James gasped.

'Nor can I,' whispered Anna. 'I can't get my breath.'

They slumped down at the side of the path. For long minutes they sat, their bodies shuddering with the effort of breathing.

'I should think we've only climbed about seventy metres in half an hour,' Anna said when her breathing had calmed sufficiently for her to be able to speak. 'If we progress at this rate it will be dark before we get near the hut.'

'If it's even there.'

'If it isn't there we'll have to set about building some sort of shelter to keep the rain off. If we get soaked and then have to spend the night in the open we'll be suffering from exposure before we know it, as well as altitude sickness.'

James stood and gathered up his rucksack again.

'What we did on the Ruwenzori expedition when we found ourselves in difficulties was to climb twenty steps, stop and count to one hundred slowly, then do another twenty. In the end that's quicker than exhausting yourself and spending half an hour recovering. "Slow but sure" I think is the plan now.'

'And don't talk,' suggested Anna. 'Save breath.'

'Right,' James said. 'Let's try again. We'll take it really slowly.'

They started climbing again.

The mountain seemed to stretch above them to infinity.

Four hours later they had reached their physical limits.

They slumped down again, breathing with terrible effort, dragging air into their lungs with great, retching gasps.

It was several minutes before either was able to speak.

'How far do you think we've climbed?' Anna asked finally.

'I don't know. More than three hundred metres. Twice that I should think.'

'We've missed the hut then.'

'No,' James answered. 'We couldn't have missed it. It would have been a big hut, with outbuildings for the porters and the cooks. We haven't missed it. It wasn't there. This is the wrong track.'

'What now then? We can't go on, can we?' Anna observed. 'The altitude will kill us.'

'I know.' James looked exhausted and defeated.

There was a long silence as they contemplated failure, waiting for their breathing to slow and the fierce hammering of their hearts to quieten.

Anna shivered. The soft wind of lower altitudes had turned cool and was moaning through the trees. She delved into her rucksack and produced a sweater.

James got to his feet and pulled the machete out of his rucksack.

'Right,' he announced, wearily. 'We'll need a shelter for the night. It's going to be very cold before long. Tomorrow we'll have to retrace our steps and try again. It's too late to go down again now and I'm too exhausted anyway.'

He looked around. The trees close by were thick and old.

'Back in a minute,' he said.

He pushed his way through some dense growth and peered deeper into the forest. A little way off a copse of *Hypericum* sapling looked likely material to make a frame for a shelter. He made his way across and started to chop some down. The machete thudded satisfyingly into the frail wood.

Then, from somewhere below, he heard a strange noise.

He stopped and listened, momentarily alarmed.

The wind moaned, there was a slow creak and a soft thud.

He felt the hair stand up on the back of his neck.

He heard it again. Creak. Thud.

It sounded almost like . . .

'Anna,' he shouted. 'Get over here, quickly.'

There was a rustling and crashing of undergrowth and a breathless Anna joined him.

'Listen,' James said.

Creak. Thud.

They made their way down towards the noise and emerged finally into a clearing where, backing on to a wall of green vegetation, stood a large, dilapidated, corrugated-iron cabin. Streaked orange with rust, half hidden by unruly vegetation, the glass gone from its windows, deserted, forlorn, weather-beaten and drunkenly leaning, it was a sad picture of decay and dereliction. It wasn't the climbers' hut. But that didn't matter. At that moment it was the most wonderful sight on earth.

The door swung in the wind.

Creak. Thud.

They paused before they went in.

Distantly, muted by the dense forest, they thought they heard a burst of gunfire. But they were so used to the sound of guns that they simply shrugged.

Eleven

The group was feeding contentedly on a patch of thistles.

He sat on guard, and listened to their soft noises and grunts.

The fight with the dogs had weakened him terribly. The pain from his bitten hand had increased hour by hour. Now the wound was festering and it had kept him awake all night. He had tried to lick the ache away, but nothing he did would make it go. It throbbed, slow, stabbing in time with his heartbeat. He felt hot and found it hard to breathe easily, and when he walked his legs were weak.

All last night the female had moaned continuously with the pain from the injuries the dogs had inflicted. Perhaps she would die. She was sickly anyway. That was why she had become the victim of attack in the first place. She had been on her own, had fallen behind as the group had moved on, and no one had noticed.

Find yourself alone and weak and nature will show no mercy. No matter what you are.

He peered around at the group. They were temporarily at ease.

He had listened for the younger silverbacks returning during the night, but they had not come back. There had been gunfire and he had ushered the group higher up the mountain. The silverbacks would be missed, briefly. By some, perhaps mourned for a time. But life here was too hard, too precarious for the dead to be given much attention. Every ounce of strength was needed to avoid joining them.

He put them out of his mind. They would have left soon anyway. Or challenged him.

He watched the young feeding. He grunted affectionately as one of the female infants struggled inexpertly up a tree and collected some flowers to eat from a high vine. She painstakingly descended one-handed, holding her prized delicacy in the other. Immediately a bullying blackback rushed across, grunted in rapid staccato and attempted to grab the food from her. The frightened infant howled and struggled to keep hold of it.

Annoyed, he rose to his feet and knuckles, leaned forward and snarled a warning. The blackback swung his head round and faced him, opening his mouth wide in insolent defiance. There was a moment of tense stand-off as they glared at each other. He pondered whether to rush the blackback, chase him away. But, before the decision needed to be made, the blackback suddenly lowered his eyes in submission and slunk back to his former position. He was glad of that. He did not feel strong enough for a confrontation. He sat down again, grumbling. The blackbacks irritated him. They squabbled and pestered everybody. Today he felt he could not be bothered with them. He sighed and allowed his great shoulders to slump.

The group was small and ailing now. The females coughed constantly in the sodden morning fogs. Their children, already undernourished by their ailing mothers' lack of milk, picked up infections and sickened too. The silverbacks, his allies in times of danger, were gone; the blackbacks, erratic, immature, were little use in emergency.

And there was constant tension. Constant, debilitating fear. Even now, sitting quietly high on the mountain, apparently at ease, there was tension, the inescapable feeling that something was about to happen, that some catastrophe was just beyond the boundaries of sight.

Which it usually was. Hardly a day passed without a crisis.

And he was weary of it.

Instinct was telling him that things were coming to an end here.

Perhaps now it was time to move on. Gather up the group, leave this mountain altogether and look for new places, more remote from men. Safer places, better feeding grounds.

His great head nodded forward on to his chest.

But not just yet. For the moment he was too tired even to think about it. He would rest. Sleep a little, if the pain in his hand would let him.

Perhaps, this time, it was the pain which triggered the memory.

The hands hurting now, as they had hurt then, when the wire had bitten in, long ago, long, long ago.

Whatever the reason, as he dozed, as he drifted into the half-light of the mind where sleep edges reality to the side, he remembered how things had been.

And, when he awoke again, he needed to go back. He rose and set off down the mountain. He ignored the questioning chatter from the group. They would have to fend for themselves for a while.

Twelve

Anna woke first.

She lay still.

A soft morning sunlight slanted in and painted rippling rainbows on the walls of the room and on the ceiling. Dust danced above her head. The wet smells of the rainforest, the sour-sweet heaviness of leaf-rotten earth mingling with perfumed trees drifted in through the glassless window and through the gaps between walls and roof. A pale gecko skittered along a beam and disappeared into a hole, shouting defiance down at her as he went.

Chkkkkk-Chkkkkk-Chkkkkk.

Anna smiled at him. 'Chuck, chuck, yourself,' she whispered.

She stretched and yawned, luxuriating in the quiet.

Faintly, in the far distance, bell-calls of birds were softly answered by waking monkeys. And farther off still a tree cracked as a buffalo pushed it over.

Here on the mountain the terrors of the past days seemed unreal.

How, Anna wondered, *could two worlds be so different?*

The world of guns and soldiers, helicopters, destruction and mayhem, the world of nerves jangling in constant fear, that world was gone. Here, in this forest, all was peace. The loudest sound was the gentle, musical trickling of a stream close by.

She sat up and looked around.

Even in the dim light of the torch last night it had seemed that the cabin had been long unoccupied. Now in daylight that impression was confirmed. Nobody had been here for years. Everything was covered in mildew and pale-green fungal growth.

But equally obviously, the cabin had been abandoned at short notice.

Anna's gaze moved slowly around the room.

It was cluttered in an untidy, homely sort of way, its contents eccentric. The home of a person too busy to care about organization. Piles of papers and files stood next to an ancient typewriter on a 'desk' made from two packing cases with rough planks of wood nailed across them. Coffee mugs were balanced precariously on the papers, sprouting bubbling eruptions of fungus like volcanoes spewing lava. More piles of typing paper lay on the floor. A noticeboard was fastened to the wall above the desk, displaying dozens of photographs pinned haphazardly in a huge collage of memories, their subjects now faded into insipid blues and pinks, pale ghosts of time. An expensive Leica camera hung on the wall near the desk, its leather case mostly eaten away by termites, its lens white with mildew. In the typewriter a yellowing piece of paper drooped with damp, falling limply back over the carriage. The paper was accusing in its blankness and expectant readiness. It was like a small distillation of the atmosphere of the place they had come to.

Waiting, Anna thought. *That's what it is. The room's waiting.*

The rotting books on the shelves; the coffee pot with a large enamel mug still beside it on the wood-burning stove; the big, blackened cooking-pans on a makeshift rack; the tinned food, labels stained with age and damp, in the open-fronted cupboard; the plates and cutlery on the table; all were waiting for someone who never came back.

A soft snuffling and shuffling from outside the cabin made Anna jump. But it was followed immediately by the snort of a bush pig. She smiled to herself.

James woke and yawned.

'What was that?' he asked, sleepily.

'Just a foraging pig. Amazing, isn't it? This place looks as though it's been empty for years, and as soon as people arrive the opportunists start rolling up.'

'So long as that's all that rolls up.'

Anna stood up. She looked through the window, out on to a large clearing. Tree stumps overgrown with emerald green mosses were dotted here and there and the grass was waist-high. But the forest had not gained too much of a hold and the tree stumps, poisoned into submission, had sent up only slender, tired-looking saplings. There was a small corrugated-iron shed a few metres away from the main cabin. Flakes of green paint remained against the orange rust, evidence of the colour it had once been.

'I'm just popping outside for a minute. There's a shed over there that looks as though it may have been a loo.'

James stood and looked out too. 'I wouldn't risk any sheds. You never know what might be in them.'

'Hmm, if I scream, rescue me.'

The door creaked as Anna opened it and more sunlight flooded into the room.

A few minutes later she returned.

'It *is* a loo, with an old chemical toilet in it. It's all right. No snakes or anything. Isn't this a weird place? Everything's just left as though someone will walk back into it. There's a pile of logs near the shed over there, with a rusty axe still embedded in one.'

'Good,' said James. 'I'll see if I can get this stove going. We might think about staying here a day or two, until we see whether Dominic can get help. A rest would help us acclimatize too.'

'Hmm! And we might find something edible in this lot,' Anna observed, inspecting the rows of tinned food. 'I don't suppose baked beans go off no matter how old they are.' She held a dark brown jar with a rusted lid up to the light. 'This was coffee once,' she said. She unscrewed the lid and smelled inside. 'Well, it still smells of coffee. It's all caked together but it might serve its purpose.'

'Wonderful,' James said. 'Baked beans and coffee. All we need is some bacon. Go and see if you can catch that bush pig.'

'You catch it. I'm going to set about cleaning the mould off the plates, it looks as though it could be fatal. There's a stream just over there. I could hear it trickling. I'll get some water.'

Anna picked up one of the large cooking pans and they went out together. James scrutinized the axe, pronounced it blunt but not too blunt and set about splitting some of the smaller logs.

Anna walked to the edge of the clearing and then

into the denser bush. She followed the sound of the stream and found that it was only ten metres or so into the forest, running in the bottom of a narrow gully. It burbled gently over moss-covered rocks. It smelled sweet and fresh and clean. The light was very subdued, dappled, and as Anna picked her way down the slope she stumbled occasionally, mistaking shadows for rocks. Soft bird-calls whispered from deeper in the forest, muted by the festoons of feathery mosses hanging from the trees. Even the dull clack of James's axe quickly faded away.

Ten metres from the hut she was in another world.

She reached the stream, sat down by its side and put the pan underneath a rock from which a thin, but steady, trickle of water flowed. The water pattered metallically against the bottom of the pan. She sighed contentedly and looked around.

A great *Hagenia* tree, gnarled and tattered, leaned precariously over the stream a little way away, its long purple flowers almost glowing in the muted light. She allowed her eyes to drift slowly up its massive trunk, marvelling at the assortment of ferns and mosses and orchids which had made their homes upon its friendly bark. She wondered for how long this tree had been standing here. Decades? Centuries? Had the vanished occupant of the cabin sat here where she was sitting, marvelling and asking the same question?

Her eyes drifted down again to the tree's base, where a great mattress of mosses had grown. And then to the side of the tree.

Her brow furrowed in puzzlement. A row of moss-covered humps, each about half a metre high and set at regular intervals, angled away from the tree. She counted them. Five. Five almost identical humps. Too evenly spaced, it seemed, to be natural. Curious, she rose and made her way cautiously down to them, wading through the stream.

Each hump was about a metre from the other. She knelt at the first and started to scrape away the moss. The domed top of a stone was revealed. A shaped stone, bearing the unmistakable marks of a chisel. She moved her hand down to the front of the stone and pulled the moss away from there. There were words

POOR CLYDE
1964

Intrigued she moved to the next and scraped the moss from that too.

MWEEZI
1965

The lettering was uneven, amateur. But it was carefully, painstakingly, carved.

Anna shook her head in wonderment.

Gravestones. Here, in the rainforest, in this beautiful place, on this most remote, impenetrable of mountains.

She sat down beside the stones and decided not to touch any more of them.

So very strange, she thought as she sat pondering them. *What lives had been lived and ended here? Who was Clyde and what thing had happened to him, so terrible that he became, perhaps in life but certainly in death, 'poor' Clyde?*

And what had he and Mweezi, 'the thief', been?

Suddenly Anna felt a great sadness sweep over her.

She found herself, in an instant, to be weeping quietly. Not for whoever, *whatever*, lay beneath the gravestones. They were long gone and unknown to her, though their sad ghosts had triggered her tears. The stones spoke eloquently of love and loss. She wept for herself and for James and Alfred and her parents. For the terrors of the past days and fear of the future. For their way of life now irretrievably gone, for the destructive stupidity of people and for sad Rwanda's descent into ruin. For all the thousand things that whirled around in her brain, without form or focus, all piercingly sad.

The pan was overflowing. Anna picked it up and headed back to the cabin. As she climbed back up the gully slope she thought she heard a noise from somewhere behind her. A sound so soft it could almost have been a dove cooing. She stopped, turned and stared. She saw nothing, of course. The forest is shadows laid upon shadows. But she knew someone, *something*, was there in the mysterious, curtained, green caverns between the trees.

As she turned away and resumed her climb, she felt eyes upon her back.

Thirteen

'*Stories of the Gorilla Country.*' Anna lifted the book down from the makeshift bookshelf. She opened it. 'By someone called Du Chaillu. Printed in 1867.'

She riffled through the pages.

An airmail envelope fell out. She picked it up and examined it. Like the book it was stained with age and damp.

'From Doctor Jane Hudson, PO Box 29, Ruhengeri.'

'What?' James asked.

'This letter. She must have been using it as a bookmark and then forgotten to post it. It's from a Doctor Hudson, addressed to a Professor David Hudson, at Cambridge University.'

She replaced it and put the book back on the shelf. Then she walked over to the desk and cast her eyes over the accumulation of papers on its surface. 'It's almost as though she could walk back in at any minute, sit down here in this chair and continue her typing. Wherever she went, she obviously intended to do just that. Even loaded her typewriter with a new piece of paper. I wonder what happened to her?'

A diary lay next to the typewriter. Anna picked it up and opened it.

Then she closed it and put it down again.

'I feel a bit guilty,' she said. 'Prying into someone else's affairs.'

'Oh, I don't think she'd mind.' James smiled. 'Wherever she went, she never came back, and it might explain what happened to her.'

'All right.'

She opened it and began to read out loud.

'June 3rd 1966,' she began.

June 3rd 1966
Shasha Camp

The survivors of Group 3 were still in great agitation yesterday.

Juvenal and I called out as we approached them, but they were still so traumatized by the attack they would not allow us near them. There was a great deal of anxious screaming and threatening and they moved on ahead of us. I think they will never, because we are human, trust us again.

I now believe it would have been better if I had never come here. All my efforts, destroying traps, filling in the pits, stopping the locals killing the gorillas for meat and encroaching on their habitat, all have made things worse. This attack on Group 3 was revenge on me. They dare not kill me so they have destroyed the thing dearest to me; my life's work. Doctor Brendel predicted that there would be no mountain gorillas left by the year 2000. That they would become extinct in the same century they were discovered. My interference in their lives has made that prediction more likely to be fulfilled.

This is the final straw. I can no longer stay here. I will write to my father and tell him I am coming home. And at the weekend I will begin to pack.

But first I must find Shadow. I cannot leave without saying goodbye to him.

Anna closed the diary and replaced it on the desk.

'She never packed.' She gestured around the room. 'All her belongings are still here. Even clothes in the other room. She just left and never came back.'

'That letter might be the one she mentions. The one to her father.' James said. He crossed to the bookshelf and retrieved the letter. 'I'm going to open it.'

He tore open the envelope.

'No, it's older. The date is much earlier. 1964.'

He began to read.

Shasha Camp,
PO Box 29,
Ruhengeri.
10 September 1964

My dear Father,
Your letter arrived last week. I am glad to hear you are well. But you must stop worrying about me! I have made myself a life here. I no longer feel as threatened as I did. The men are very protective of me and the gorillas accept me completely now. I am in no danger.

I will confess however that hearing all the news from Cambridge made me a little homesick. I have been somewhat depressed these last few weeks.

I have not seen Shadow now for over a month!

When Juvenal and I first named him two years ago it was because he survived – he emerged from under the Shadow of Death. But later he lived up to his name and became my shadow. Now that he is gone I am lost. The hut seems so empty without him sleeping by the stove. When I return from days in the field and he is not here, my heart sinks. At night I find it difficult to concentrate on writing up my daily reports, I worry about him so. I think he is having a difficult time establishing himself. Juvenal says he saw Group 5 making their way down to the ravine about three weeks ago. Shadow was following behind at a respectful distance. The dominant male Clyde, who I told you in my last letter was badly injured falling into a spiked pit, is getting weaker and weaker. His injuries have turned very nasty and he will not allow me near him any more. It is a great tragedy. He was at the pinnacle of his life, so fit and strong. Now he is weak and, I fear, will not last much longer. What will happen to Shadow when poor Clyde dies is anybody's guess. It was Clyde who signalled Shadow's acceptance. When he is gone there will be a power struggle between the two silverback pretenders Brutus and Cassius. Whoever wins, Shadow may find himself no longer welcome.

We'll see.

Whatever happens he won't come back here again now, except for his brief visits. If I were honest I would have to say that he drifted away from me quite quickly towards the end. That is, of course, quite natural and something for which we had all hoped fervently – that he would find his rightful place.

I do miss him though! I look forward to him turning up. There's no pattern to his visits. I'll get up one morning and he'll be sitting outside in the clearing, waiting for me. And we'll hug and play a little and he'll stay an hour or two then go again.

I think that, just now and then, he remembers me and needs to check that I'm still here. I expect that his visits will become less and less frequent as he matures and eventually he will forget about me altogether. That will be the best for him but will be a sad day for me.

I hope he succeeds in his independent life. I have taught him all I know. Shown him the traps the poachers lay, the pits they dig. We made it a game. He developed a liking for jam sandwiches, so I trained him by reward. We would go out on expeditions destroying traps together. Every time Shadow found a trap he got a sandwich. He became very adept at spotting the signs and seemed to take pleasure in destroying traps himself. In a way he has had a better preparation for survival from me than he would have done by remaining in his group. Gorillas will instinctively assist any of their kind caught in a trap. They will try to release snares and help any who fall into pits, but I have only rarely seen them actually destroying traps. They keep a watchful eye out for them but tend only to skirt round them when they find them. Shadow, I think, from my example will always destroy them now.

It is impossible however to teach him the one lesson that he needs to know above all others. Or at least I can think of no way of teaching him this.

That he must never, never approach any other humans.

I worry about this constantly now. Shadow has learned to trust Juvenal and me. Perhaps in the long run we may have done him a disservice.

Sometimes I wish that I could take your advice and not become so involved.

The greater the involvement the greater the possibility of getting hurt!

My love to you.
Jane.

'So things haven't progressed very far since 1964. People are still shooting things,' Anna sighed.

'That's true. But at least she wasn't right about the gorillas being extinct by the year 2000. There are some left.' He stood and walked over to the window. 'She was very upset when she wrote that diary entry, wasn't she? I wonder what had happened exactly? And I'd like to know about Shadow. Is there more in her diary?'

Anna turned back a few pages. She studied them for a moment.

'Are you quite sure you want to know?' she asked eventually.

James nodded.

'May 27th 1966,' Anna read.

May 27th 1966
Shasha Camp.

We returned tonight.

Group 3 is torn apart and cannot recover.

The two infants, trusting Nods and shy, little Sammy, have gone. Perhaps they have been taken alive, for sale. Their father, gentle Samson, poor Clyde's son, who allowed Nods and Sammy to sit on my knee, we found curled up at the foot of a Hagenia tree. He had crawled there and died from his bullet wounds. Died protecting his family. As had his son, the silverback Brutus, who would have succeeded him. As had the two blackbacks Gog and Magog whose bodies were also close by. There is now no successor (the senior bloodline male was Uncle Remus who died of pneumonia last year).

The females have fled. Juvenal says he saw Kuku carrying

her dead baby. They may now vacate Muhavura altogether and move to Sabinio or Gahinga. There is, I would guess, no future wherever they go. This line will now die out. They are gone.

And I grieve for them.

'I can't stop thinking about it,' Anna said. 'It's been on my mind all afternoon.'

They were standing outside the cabin, looking up the mountain. The first shadows of dusk were beginning to gather. The afternoon rains had finished and the forest smelled sweet and clean. Birds muttered sleepily to each other. Distant, agitated monkeys were engaged in arguments over sleeping places.

A dark bateleur eagle sailed majestically into view above their heads. With a single beat of massive wings it came to a halt and remained motionless, pinned to a cloud by a shaft of sunlight. Then it stooped, fell like a stone from the sky, snatched an invisible prey out of the air and soared, in seconds, to such great height it vanished from sight.

'Mine too,' said James. 'I'm going for some water. Just for something to do. Shut the picture out of my mind.'

'I'll come with you,' Anna said.

They made their way down to the stream. The last of the golden sunlight was beginning to redden. The forest was bathed in a gentle, diffused light, caught between colours, fading from one to the other. The light imbued it with a magical, theatrical air, the enchanted forest of childhood pantomime.

James positioned the pan in the stream, then walked over to the gravestones.

Anna sat quietly watching the soft sunlight play on the trees and dance among the hanging mosses. Shadows moved, changed shape and colour and texture, as the light shifted. Her eyes drifted out to where the forest was denser, less distinct. To where the reddening light of sunset filtered only dimly, where the trees and vines were a black latticework against fire-glow. To where a deeper shadow than the others caught her attention. A shadow more profound than any other. A shadow darker than dark, blacker than black.

She fancied it moved. Or was it just a trick of the light?

Frowning, she stood and stared hard at it.

'James,' she called softly.

'What?'

'There's something there.'

'Where?'

'By that big tree. To the right of it. In the tree's shadow . . .'

Shadow.

A lifetime since a gentle human voice had spoken his name.

The gorilla grunted softly at the word, puzzled.

Shadow.

It echoed somehow in his mind, recalled something. Nothing clear, it was all too long ago for that. Impressions. A feeling of how things had once been, here, at this place. A sense of safety and trust long gone and of the figures who had once been here and touched his life.

A fleeting call from a long-dead ghost of time.

He stepped out from beside the tree and went forward to investigate.

Later they would remember the reddening sun dancing on his night-black pelt. Would remember the strange, shuffling gait, head and shoulders swaying as the knuckles of one hand thudded into the ground, the other hand held high. Recall the strong musky odour; and the great, leathery face, so different yet so strangely familiar, so animal yet so nearly human. And the eyes, full of enquiry and intelligence.

But that was later. When he had gone.

All they felt at the time, as this great creature approached them, was shock. His emergence from the shadows was so sudden, his presence so darkly massive and powerful, that James and Anna instinctively stepped back, preparing themselves for flight.

The gorilla stopped and stared at them, pivoting its head from side to side uneasily, as though trying to decide their intentions.

And, because they too were uneasy and unable to define *his* intentions, James and Anna took a further step back.

The gorilla stared with increased concentration, then shook his head once and grunted softly.

Wuh . . . wuh . . . wuh.

'That's the sound I heard this morning,' Anna whispered. 'It was him watching me then.' She studied him carefully and found no threat in his gaze, only puzzlement, enquiry. 'He doesn't intend us any harm, I'm sure.' Hesitantly she stepped towards him.

His eyes flicked from her to James and back. He put his head on one side again and stared hard at her face. Then, suddenly, his brow wrinkled into a frown and he growled.

'What?' Anna whispered. 'What is it?'

The gorilla shook his head, snorted, then turned and started to move away.

Anna took a step after him.

'No,' she called, 'don't go. It's all right. Don't go.'

He did not pause.

'Wait. Please.'

But he didn't.

Momentarily, without breaking his step, he turned his head and looked over his shoulder.

Then the forest shadows folded him into themselves and he was gone.

Fourteen

'James, are you awake?'

'Yes.'

'Listen. He's still doing it.'

Muffled by distance, the eerie cry.

OOOOOM-AAAAAGH.

OOOOOM-AAAAAGH.

'What time is it?'

The torch flickered on and then off again. Its beam, momentarily illuminating the interior of the cabin, made the subsequent darkness more profound.

'Quarter to five. Be getting light soon. He's been doing that on and off all night. I've woken a few times and heard him. The same sound, over and over again. I never heard anything so lonely,' she whispered. 'Not ever in my life did I hear anything so lonely or sad. He's like a wolf howling at the moon.'

'I know.'

'He wanted something,' Anna continued. 'I've no idea what it could be. But I know he wanted something from us. The way he stared at me it was almost as though he thought he knew me.'

'He wanted to come closer. But for some reason didn't.'

'I know. I felt a bit sorry for him somehow. All that incredible power and strength and *I* felt sorry for *him*.'

'I can't understand what made him come near us. These poor creatures have been hunted almost to extinction. Why would he approach us? You would think he'd run a mile at the sight of humans.'

'I don't know. It's all very mysterious. Did you notice his hand? The way he walked towards us – he wasn't using one of his hands. He couldn't put it down on the ground. He's injured. Perhaps that was what he wanted from us. Help.'

'Help? What help could we possibly be? And why would a gorilla look to humans for help. It's about the last thing they'd expect.'

'I don't know. One thing I do know, I was sad for him. Something in his eyes made me sad. I don't know why but my heart went out to him and I think he knew it, sensed something that made a real contact between us. Then all of a sudden he closed up.'

'Perhaps you weren't what he was expecting.'

'What on earth could a gorilla be *expecting*?'

'I don't know. Let's try and get a bit more sleep before morning.'

Morning sun flooded into the room. James had lit a fire in the stove. The burning wood crackled cheerfully and sweet wisps of smoke leaked into the room, perfuming it. A pan of rice was bubbling away and a frying pan hissed and sizzled happily next to it. They had found a tin of cooking oil and Anna was frying the last of the bread they had bought at Kidaho.

The lingering effects of altitude, the niggling headaches and nausea, were rapidly receding. Things were getting better!

'We'll be able to move on by ourselves soon, if Dominic doesn't come,' James said. He was poking around the room inspecting its cluttered contents. 'We won't find the altitude so difficult now.' He lifted the lid of an old metal trunk. 'Hey, look at this.'

'What?'

'More diaries. In this box. It's filled with old diaries.' He picked one out. It was white with mildew, heavy with damp.

'Pass one here,' Anna said, as she poked the frying bread around the pan.

'They're not in bad condition given their age. This one's 1962.'

Anna took the book and opened it. On the inside of the cover, in slightly blurred ink, was written

Shasha Camp – Parc des Volcans.

This book is the property of Doctor
Jane Hudson. If found please return it
to her via Post Office Box 29, Ruhengeri,
Rwanda, or if that is not possible to
Professor David Hudson, at the University
of Cambridge, England.
Thank you.

She tried to open the first pages. January, February, March were glued together, made inseparable by decades of damp. April and May were better, but as the pages peeled apart they stuck in places, tore and became illegible. June and July, protected in the centre of the book were in the best condition.

Anna started to read. 'June 20th 1962, Shasha

Camp, midnight.' Then after a moment or two, 'James? I think we'd better eat first. There's a lot to read.'

Later she began to read out loud.

June 20th 1962

Today the porters came back from town in great excitement.

As they approached the camp they were calling out to the cook that they had a gift for 'Mama', as they call me.

The Head Porter, Juvenal, was carrying a sack on his back. He laid it gently down in front of me, untied it and tipped its contents out at my feet.

A ball of jet-black fur, about the size of a football, rolled out on to the ground and lay, absolutely motionless, at my feet. They had found a baby gorilla.

At first I thought he was dead but then I noticed the fingers of one hand part and a small, brown eye peeked at me fearfully. I knelt down and tried to reassure him. He began to tremble. He was, I guess, at the end of his tether, half dead from whatever terrible ordeal he had endured.

Perhaps sensing that he had found a friend, he rolled on to his feet, put his arms round my neck and his legs round my waist and clung on for dear life. He clings to me now as I write.

June 21st 1962

Morning.
Gorillas weep! Real tears! I didn't know.

The foundling stayed with me all night, clinging to me, though there was hardly room on the camp bed for both of us. Sometimes he dozed, sometimes he just clung to me and whimpered, but sometimes he sobbed and wept and my neck became wet with his tears.

I tried to separate us but it was no good. When I tried to remove his arms from my neck he screamed. I think his wrists are injured. Perhaps they have been bound with wire.

Juvenal doesn't know how he came to be where he was. One of the porters spotted him sleeping in the shadows at the foot of a tree and threw a sack over him before he could get away. No doubt the poor thing is the survivor of some terrible event. Destined for a zoo perhaps and escaped?

Evening.
Some success! The gorilla let go of me.

I sent Juvenal out to collect some celery and Galium vine which are the staple diet of young gorillas. He put it down in the doorway and I took the cub over to see it. I knelt down and he put out his hand and patted the food then put his arm back round my neck. He kept looking fearfully at Juvenal so I sent him away. Alone with me the animal became more confident and eventually he let go of me and started to eat. He must have been at least partially weaned by his mother. If that had not been the case then there would have been no hope of his survival.

When he finished eating he sat and stared at me for many minutes.

He has the most beautiful soft brown eyes, deep and intelligent, but very, very wary. His fur is still fluffy. I guess him to be between two and three years old. A male. Quite fit, I think.

So – good news at the moment. If we had some dried milk things would be more hopeful. There is milk, I hear, in Kisoro, but no one can cross to Uganda.

The cub is sitting on my lap as I write. He watches my pen move across the page. Sometimes his hand raises a little as though he wants to join in. There are wire noose marks on his wrists, so I think his hands hurt as he lifts them. Perhaps when he is more confident I will be able to treat his wounds.

Tomorrow we'll organize food-gathering for him. It's too early yet to talk about survival, but we may be able to find out where he came from and perhaps return him there.

I'm hopeful.

As I watched him eating I think I detected a will to live. Whatever the trauma he has endured he may be strong enough to come through it!

June 25th 1962

The gorilla suddenly gave up the fight. I think his courage ran out.

I am not surprised. I know what happened – Juvenal found a witness. As I guessed, he was captured by zoo hunters. The witness, a MuTutsi tribesman, says hunters came on to the mountain seeking an infant male and simply shot all the rest of the group to get him. So this infant witnessed his entire family die. And then they dragged him down the mountain with wires on his wrists. When Juvenal cut the wires off he found they were embedded in his flesh. Anyway it appears the hunters had rounded a corner and walked straight into a herd of buffalo. The buffalo scattered them and gored a couple. The MuTutsi found their bodies in the bush at the side of the path.

I suppose the cub escaped then.

Now the trauma has just proved too much. Yesterday he let go of me, ignored his food and went and sat in a corner of the hut. He has been there ever since. I've put some water down for him to drink but he hasn't touched it. His eyes have lost their life. He's dying, I think.

June 29th 1962

Juvenal has had an idea. He has made a sort of papoose out of bits of wood and an old canvas water bucket. Today he marched into the hut and shook it at me and gestured at the cub.

'Tomorrow we find gorillas. I carry him,' he announced.

It may work. Contact with his own kind may bring back some interest in life. But it could also be dangerous. For him and us.

I think he may be beyond help now. He is curled up in the foetal position, asleep. Perhaps he won't wake up again.

I am fighting my involvement with him. His death is hurting me, even though he has been here so short a time. He seems so small and defenceless and damaged. Even silent and motionless he is worming into my heart. Obviously into Juvenal's too.

July 1st 1962
Mount Muhavura

Tonight I write in an abandoned poachers' den, an ikibooga, built into the hollow bole of an ancient Hagenia. These trees are very common in the forest. This one is about three metres across. Its branches are covered with bright orchids and the entire tree is festooned with long wispy strands of mosses and lichens. They remind me of fairy-tale wizards, benign, forgetful, old souls covered with cobwebs and spiders.

The hollowed trunk still has evidence of its last occupants. There are a few wire snares and some pieces of dried antelope meat wrapped in leaves lying around. But I think it is many months, years perhaps, since anyone was here. The snares are so rusted they crumble and flake in your hands and the dried meat is white with mildew.

It is warm and dry and comfortable in the bole of the tree and the vanilla smell of the purple flowers mingles with the sweet wood-smoke of the fire. It is very peaceful and beautiful up here on Muhavura's slopes. This is a holy mountain. The Rwandans believe that the souls of the good will come here for eternity. Certainly this forest is as close to heaven as I have found, though high on the mountain top, where Rwanda meets Uganda, it is barren and hail-scoured.

Juvenal is cradling Shadow (as we have agreed to call him). They sit together by the fire as I write, the gorilla asleep in Juvenal's arms. Juvenal is very proud of what he has done. I could never have carried the cub up here, he is far too heavy for me. Too heavy for Juvenal too, I suspect, but he did not complain once, rested hardly ever and refused offers of help from the other porters.

An astonishing thing has occurred. We trekked for most of the first day, up to the point on the mountain where we had last seen a gorilla group. We quickly found fairly fresh night-nests so knew a group was in the area, though saw none of them. If gorillas choose not to be found then they know how to vanish – even if you are close to them. But we felt their presence. No one said anything, but the porters became uneasy, glancing over their shoulders and peering into the depths of the forest.

Shadow, who until now had lolled listlessly in his papoose, barely seeming to be awake, or even sometimes, I thought, alive, lifted his head and began to take an interest in his surroundings. He too peered carefully into the forest and occasionally gave little grunts very similar to purring. Or rather a cross between purring and burping! It was the first sound of contentment I had heard him make. He did this for about half an hour then the presence left us. We all felt their departure, though nobody remarked upon it. The porters relaxed and Shadow slept again.

As dusk approached we found the ikibooga and settled down for the night. Juvenal and the porters gathered leaves for our beds before darkness fell. We made our nests in other words! Then they lit a fire and cooked some soup.

Juvenal even climbed a Pygeum tree and brought Shadow some of the fruits. He ignored them and crept up to me and nestled against me. His breathing had become shallow and his movements slow.

We fell asleep together.

And, as far as I was concerned, I fell asleep convinced that it had all been a waste of time.

This, I was certain, would be Shadow's last night.

He would die quietly, in the night, beside me. Of heartbreak. And tomorrow we would go back down the mountain without him.

I was wrong.

Several times in the night I awoke and found him still breathing, but each time it was a surprise. I stroked his head a little each time but he showed no reaction. I felt that he was in the sleep of death and that he would drift away from us without ever waking.

Finally I fell into a deep sleep, from which I was woken, by Juvenal, just after dawn. He was whispering, 'Mama, Mama', and was obviously worried. The other two porters were standing fearfully a few metres away holding their spears at the ready.

'Look, Mama, Look. Look at Shadow,' one of them said.

I looked around trying to gather my senses and found to my delight that Shadow was not only alive but was sitting a few metres away from us happily munching on what appeared to be a huge mushroom!

I went over and sat beside him. The life-light had returned to his eyes and he grunted at me. Then he turned his back on me, possessively hugged his food, and continued to munch away at it.

For a minute or two I was at a loss to know why Juvenal and the porters were fearful.

But then I realized. What Shadow was eating was a newly broken-off bracket fungus. This is a parasite that grows high on the trunks of the Hagenia trees. It is quite rare and is a great favourite of gorillas. But it is so firmly fixed to the trees that it requires very great strength, more than human strength and certainly much more than any healthy infant gorilla's strength, to break it away.

Even supposing Shadow had had the strength to climb a tree, which he certainly did not, he would not have been able to harvest this.

So – the conclusion is – and this was why the men were afraid – we had a visitor, or visitors, in the night.

Bearing gifts!

They know we are here and they know we have Shadow! They have sensed that he is ill and have done what they would have done if he had been a sickly infant in their own group: they have brought him food. One of them must have overcome his, or more likely her, fear of us to do this.

So here we are at the end of the second night.

Shadow has, I believe, passed the crisis. He has gathered in strength throughout the day. He has shown interest in the forest and has now and then ventured a few metres into it. But he is very nervous. He returns to Juvenal and me very quickly.

He knows his own kind are out there though. Of that I have no doubt. I feel them to be there too.

Watching us.

But they have made no sound all day. The forest is as quiet as a grave.

I have made the decision that we will stay and see what happens. I have sent the Tutsi porters back to the cabin for more food. They made no effort to conceal their delight to be leaving. They are terrified of gorillas. Gorilla groups have been known to attack villages, smashing doors of huts down in concerted, obviously planned attacks to retrieve stolen infants. So the men think that Juvenal and I are in mortal danger here.

This group however will know that this infant is not theirs. So I do not think we are in danger at all.

We'll see who is right eventually, I suppose.

Juvenal says little, so I do not know what he thinks. But he has stayed!

And Shadow trusts him!

See what tomorrow brings . . .

July 4th 1962

Back at camp!

We came down today, arriving just before dark.

Events both wonderful and terrible have happened. I don't know how to interpret them with regard to Shadow's future.

We hoped, of course, that some contact with his own kind would rekindle his interest in living. That has undoubtedly worked. But there are worries now for the longer term.

109

We waited all of Monday for something to happen. Nothing much did. Shadow filled his day munching his fungus and listening intently to the goings on in the forest. A gorilla's hearing is at least ten times better than ours, so although I could hear little, Shadow could obviously hear a lot. Occasionally he made attempts at communication, peering into the forest and making soft mewing sounds. Once he screamed and chattered, but I don't think received an answer. The day passed like this, but we noticed that he returned to Juvenal and me for reassurance less frequently throughout the day. By late afternoon he seemed to have become more accustomed to his surroundings and even began to make efforts at building a nest a few metres away from the base of the tree, as though he intended spending the night close to us but not actually wrapped round us as he has been doing. He began bending Senecio stalks down to the ground. But every time he let one go it sprang back up again. He puzzled about it for a while, then tried holding stalks down with his feet while he bent others down with his hands. But the same thing happened. As soon as he let go, the woody stalks shot back up again and he would stand for a while grumbling at them under his breath and occasionally tossing handfuls of soil at them.

Then he got frustrated and angry and the grumbling became screams and he pranced around the failed nest, bouncing up and down on all four limbs like a furry ball, eventually throwing himself on his back on the Senecio and lying there waving his legs in the air. It was so funny to watch that Juvenal and I laughed out loud. At which he got up, abandoned his nest entirely and came over and snuggled into my arms. 'Why go to all that bother?' you could almost hear him say.

BUT – the point is, he was doing normal things. The

110

routine of his previous life was beginning to re-establish itself.

Juvenal was right. Taking Shadow up there has saved his life.

Yesterday, however, brought a set-back.

Shadow started the day making forays into the forest, but remaining where he could still see us. Then, suddenly, he gathered confidence and ventured further away, out of our sight. Juvenal and I followed. We caught up with him and found him moving through the trees slowly, but with an obvious determination. He would progress a few metres, stop and listen intently, his head to one side, making small belch-like noises, as though announcing his presence or making contact. We strained our ears but could hear no reply.

This went on for more than half an hour, during which time we gradually climbed higher up the mountain. The forest here was very dense and wet and progress was very slow. Juvenal and I were soon breathless from the exertion and the heavy air.

Shadow continued up the mountain, gaining in confidence all the time. Still we heard no noise, but eventually I began to smell gorillas. A strong musky odour.

At this point Shadow made his way into a clearing and stopped. His vocalizations changed to soft whines and he sat down, lowered his head and pretended to feed on some leaves, showing by his body movements that he was submissive. We were about ten metres behind him, with a clear view of him. I signalled to Juvenal that it was a good idea for us to copy his actions, so we crouched down too.

Then we waited.

An hour passed, during which time they gradually approached. The musky smell became heavier, more pungent and eventually, from deep in the forest ahead of us, we

111

became conscious of soft rustlings. Gorillas, for all their immense size and weight, can move very quietly.

I kept my head lowered but watched from the corners of my eyes.

Very slowly, they began to appear. Not distinct at first, for the light is very subdued in the rainforest, but appearing rather as deeper shadows than the normal forest shadows. Shadows transforming slowly into presences. Here a black, hairy arm parting some branches, there the glint of soft brown eyes peering curiously from the gloom beside a tree trunk. Behind those, to the left, the sun catching the whiteness of great canine fangs as a huge mouth yawned, the nonchalance of the action designed, I guess, to show us that its owner was not afraid.

And gradually they came out into view. Warily, one by one, they emerged into the clearing and stopped at its edges.

It is hard to describe the effect these creatures have in close proximity. Suddenly time reverses. The aeons are stripped back, the layers of evolution ripped away and we see ourselves at the childhood of the world.

They are, of course, very different from the human race. They are not related to us at all.

And yet the heart says that perhaps they are!

Juvenal and I watched, hardly breathing, until eventually eight females, three with infants clinging to them, and two juveniles of, say, four to six years old, had arranged themselves at the edges of the clearing, all peering at Shadow. Their strange leathery faces showed nothing but gentle curiosity.

But behind the group, still partially concealing themselves in the forest foliage, several big, blackback males lurked. There was nothing about their demeanour to cause alarm, but somehow their presence seemed menacing. I became

112

uneasy. Gorillas have very strong blood ties. Adult males sometimes view infant males from other groups as a threat and kill them.

It was too late to think about that then, of course. Juvenal and I would be powerless to influence events.

Shadow, anyway, seemed unworried. He continued his mock feeding and the audience continued to inspect him, with frequent grunts to each other. Then, after several tense minutes, the biggest and, from her greying fur, probably the oldest of the females, decided to take matters further. She stepped forward from the group and approached Shadow.

The blackbacks found this unsettling. One of them lashed out at nearby foliage and chattered briefly. Shadow stopped feeding and stared uncertainly at the old female for a few seconds.

Then, suddenly, as though deciding he had to risk it now or never, he rolled up on to his feet and knuckles and loped sideways, crabwise, up to her. Reaching her, he whimpered, rose up on to his legs and lifted his arms, in a heart-breakingly human way, to be picked up. She reached down and allowed him to climb up into her arms.

A happy moment. But it was short-lived.

There was a brief silence and stillness as the gorilla group took in what was happening then, shockingly, having expected the males, the blackbacks, to be the danger, it was the other females who became agitated. The ones with infants began to scream and chatter and dance from one leg to the other. Their movements were strangely erratic, jerky. The blackbacks joined in the screaming too, crashing about in the forest, flailing their arms at anything within reach. The noise was indescribable, a force hammering the brain. This went on for about a minute then suddenly the child-carrying females turned, barged their way through the group and

113

plunged headlong into the forest. They collected the blackbacks as they passed and they all crashed and screamed away. We listened to their progress until the noise faded.

When we turned our attention back to the clearing the atmosphere had changed. Shadow still clung to the old female, but the remaining females had now become belligerent and threatening, circling around them, strutting stiffly, tight-lipped and wild-eyed. The old female gripped Shadow tightly and muttered back at them – placating them, I think. Suddenly two of them rushed, screaming at the old gorilla in a coordinated attack and wrested Shadow away from her. They careered around the clearing holding him by the arms and legs, pulling and tugging at him.

They were apparently battling for possession of him.

Shadow howled terribly. The old female gave chase, grabbed Shadow away from them, but dropped him. He instantly curled up in the foetal position and lay motionless, whimpering with fear. The old female spun angrily round at the other females and screamed defiance at them. This seemed to enrage them even more. They charged her and knocked her over.

And then – Juvenal could stand it no longer.

'Stay there, Mama,' he whispered.

He plunged through the vegetation, exploded out into the clearing, gave out a great bellow at the astonished gorillas and, without even breaking his step, gathered up poor little Shadow in his arms.

Taken completely by surprise the gorillas had no time to register what was happening before Juvenal had passed through them and had shot away into the forest, carrying Shadow with him.

For a few seconds the gorillas remained motionless, uncertain what to do. Then one of the group detached herself, briefly stared hard in my direction, reared up and roared at me, contemplating attack!

I turned and fled! I hurtled down the slope, barely seeing where I was going, scratching myself on thorny branches, slipping and sliding on the wet earth, falling into patches of nettles, until finally I skidded into a tree and gave myself such a knock in the side that I fell, winded, to the ground. Unable to rise, I lay gasping for breath, waiting for my pursuer to come pounding down after me and put an end to me.

But now the noise was all coming from the direction Juvenal had gone – higher up the mountain.

They had all followed him!

And such noise: murder-filled, enraged screams and roars that made the blood run cold.

Juvenal and Shadow surely, I thought, are being torn to pieces.

I lay for a little while longer, getting my breath back and waiting for the pain in my side to ease. Then, as soon as I had recovered, I got up and took my revolver from my backpack.

Gorillas are – because of the unremitting persecution they have endured from poachers – very familiar with guns. And very afraid of them.

The only possibility open to me – if I was in time – was to try to drive the gorilla group away by firing a few shots to scare them.

It was, of course, risky. Their anger could have blinded them to danger and they might have turned on me too, gun or no gun.

But I had to take the risk!

In the event, their anger worked in my favour. They didn't hear me coming.

I crept close and found that Juvenal and Shadow were up a tree, clinging to each other for dear life!

The female gorillas were clustered together a few metres away, shrieking and screaming. The blackbacks were prancing backwards and forwards, up to the base of the tree and back again, barking and pig-grunting loudly, their mouths wide open in rage, their great teeth glinting.

I released the safety-catch on the revolver in readiness and pointed the barrel skywards. I was on the point of firing when a thought crossed my mind. There had been no actual attack. Just display.

Gorillas are good climbers, but none of them were attempting to climb up to Juvenal and Shadow. Why?

I decided I could safely wait and see what happened.

I lowered the gun but kept it ready.

A few seconds later, from higher up the mountain there came a tremendous roar and a great crashing and breaking of vegetation. Immediately all activity around the tree stopped. All the gorillas moved away from the base of the tree. They stared sulkily upwards. They had apparently been given an order.

The crashing got louder and louder and eventually a huge, immensely powerful and very irritable silverback erupted into their midst. Obviously he was put out by their behaviour. He emerged at full, four-limbed, sideways gallop, hurtled, roaring with rage, across to the blackbacks and with a series of fearsome clouts around their heads and shoulders, scattered them.

Howling with humiliation, they disappeared.

The silverback paused briefly to watch them go, then turned his attention to the cowering females and infants. He slammed his knuckles down on to the ground, roared at them, then, with a stately strut, paced up and down in *front of them, never taking his eyes from them. Slowly they too crept away into the forest.*

When they were gone the silverback turned his attention to Juvenal and Shadow. He paced up to the foot of the tree and surveyed them. And although Juvenal was obviously afraid, as indeed was I, Shadow was not. After a moment or two of staring at the silverback he struggled free of Juvenal's arms and began to descend the tree.

The silverback watched calmly as Shadow came down, approached him and sat down in front of him. I held my breath. Shadow looked so tiny in front of this massive figure. So vulnerable.

And there they remained for some minutes, the silverback peering intently at him and grunting softly. Then, as abruptly as he had arrived, the silverback rose, strutted across the clearing and vanished into the trees. It was all over.

The conclusion? There is hope for the future. The silverback could have killed Shadow with one blow. If he had seen him as a threat he would have done so. Perhaps one day Shadow may be accepted by the group.

We will try again when he is a little older.

'Do you think it could be him? Could it be Shadow?' Anna put the book down. She raised her head and listened.

The sad cry still rolled periodically down the slopes.

'I suppose it could be,' James replied. 'I wish he'd stop doing that, it's boring into my head.'

'That would certainly explain why a gorilla would approach humans. He's used to them.' She furrowed her brows. 'Except it was all a very long time ago.'

'1962,' James said. 'That would make him in his

forties now, if it is him. Do you think an animal would remember for that long?'

'We remember things all our lives. I suppose animals do too. Is forties old, I wonder, for a gorilla?'

'Very, I think.'

'He looked old,' Anna continued. 'Perhaps that's why he seemed so sad to me. He looked defeated when he turned away, really. Dragging his hand, poor thing.'

James walked over to the door and looked out.

'I wonder what happened to Doctor Hudson?' he mused. 'She obviously loved this place and her work.'

'And Shadow. She loved Shadow,' Anna added. 'I wonder if she ever got to say goodbye to him. It seems she never returned after she set out to find him. At least there's no evidence of any more writing after that date – so I assume she never returned.'

'I don't think there's much point in pursuing that mystery,' James said. 'It wasn't solved when it happened, it's far too late now.'

'If anybody tried to solve it.' Anna gestured round the room. 'Nobody's been here, that's obvious. You'd think things would be disturbed. If people had searched for her you'd think they'd start here.'

'Forget it, Anna, that's my advice,' James said. 'It's too far in the past. What happened, happened. Apparently nothing could change it then. Nothing can make any difference now. It all finished long ago.'

OOOOOM-AAAAAGH.

The cry floated down to them through the trees.

Anna joined James at the doorway. She looked up the mountainside, to where the morning sun pulled soft wraiths of swirling mist from the trees. Looked up into the impenetrable, enchanted mystery that was the forest, to where she thought he might be. She tried to picture him again in her mind, the strangeness of him, his power and sadness, his questioning face. She shook her head.

'I'm not so sure it is finished yet.'

'What do you mean?' James asked.

'I don't know,' she said softly. 'I don't know what I mean.'

She remained in the doorway staring out across the tops of the trees for many minutes.

'But I think I need to find out.'

Fifteen

'I need to sit down a minute,' Anna gasped.

It was approaching noon and the fierce sun sucked water up out of the sodden ground and left it suspended in the air.

'Thank goodness,' James said, wiping the sweat from his face with a handkerchief. 'I need to rest too. This is like walking under water.'

They slumped down against a tree, their lungs rasping and their hearts thudding.

'It's not the altitude,' Anna observed eventually, as her tortured breathing began to slow. 'I don't feel sick or anything. It's just the humidity. We aren't built to get oxygen from water.'

James nodded. 'I don't think we've actually climbed all that much anyway,' he said. 'We've been traversing the mountain mainly. I'd guess we're no more than 200 metres higher than we were at the cabin. It just feels like we've climbed a long way with all the dead-ends and backtracking we've had to do.'

'Dominic said it's called the Impenetrable Forest on the Ugandan side,' Anna mused.

'Hmm. Let's just hope we don't run into any of the returning Tutsi that he said lived there.'

In the distance the gorilla called again.

'There he goes again.' James got to his feet. 'He

still sounds a long way off. I hope what we're doing is sensible.'

'Of course it's not sensible. To be honest I don't know why we're doing it at all. We should be getting out of this country while we still can and finding Mum and Dad, not chasing after some gorilla. I just have the feeling that it's one of those things that if we don't do, we'll regret for the rest of our lives. We'll always wonder what would have happened if . . .' Anna got to her feet too. She rummaged in James's rucksack and produced the bottle of water. 'Do you know what I mean?'

'Strangely enough, I know exactly what you mean.' James looked around briefly, selected a nearby tree to act as a trail-marker and with two swift blows of the machete hacked a neat wedge out of it. The cut seeped a milky liquid which began a glutinous progress down the trunk. Immediately a long line of ants appeared, as if by magic, at the base of the tree and began to climb towards the oozing fluid.

'How far do you think we've come?' Anna asked, pondering the ant-line's urgency with mild interest.

'I don't know really. I've lost count of the trees I've marked. A hundred perhaps, most at about ten metres. Say a kilometre. Perhaps a little more.'

'It feels like ten times that. And he still sounds almost as far away as he was. I hope he doesn't decide to leave when he hears us coming.'

'I expect he knows we're coming already. Knows exactly where we are and what we're doing. And sound is very deceptive in the forest. He may not be as far away as he seems.' James hoisted his rucksack up on to his shoulders. 'OK? Shall we get going again? Got your breath back now?'

'Yes. Let's go.'

James took up position in front of Anna and they resumed their slow progress.

'What time is it?' Anna asked.

'Just after noon. We've been about two hours to here. If we don't find him in the next hour we'll have to think about turning back. We should aim to be back at the cabin by six. It will be getting too dark to see the marker trees any time after that. I don't fancy a night under a makeshift shelter.'

'Nor me.'

It was the smell that they noticed first. Pungent and foul. The unmistakable smell of death. But mixed with something else. Woodsmoke perhaps. Cooking. Then the sound. A low continuous hum getting louder as they ascended.

'What's that?' James asked.

'Sounds like flies buzzing,' Anna replied. She turned her head in the direction of the sound. 'Over there. Shall we investigate?'

'All right,' James notched a tree with his machete.

They turned and followed the sound.

It led them to a clearing where a fire smouldered gently. Some bones with vestiges of meat still clinging to them littered the ground close to the fire. An arrangement of wooden poles had been rigged up to make a spit and a long piece of meat remained on it, charred black.

They looked round nervously. Whoever had been here was not long gone and intended to return. An assortment of wire snares had been hung on a tree branch and an old army coat lay close by them.

'Poachers,' said James, softly.

'Yes.'

Their eyes scanned the clearing. The buzz of flies was coming from the far side. In the trees.

'The meat on the spit,' said Anna. Her voice was strained with shock, her face white with horror. 'Look at it.'

James looked closely.

He turned away immediately. It was clearly the lower part of an arm. The fire had tightened the sinews of the hand, curving the fingers and thumb into a claw as though they reached out to grasp something.

Anna started to cross the clearing.

'Don't,' said James. 'Don't look. There's no point.'

Anna continued and entered the tree line. 'I have to,' she whispered.

James followed. He felt sick to the stomach.

One of the gorillas, the one the poachers had started to dismember and eat, was covered in flies. A simmering, humming mass of them.

Sickened, Anna waved her arms as she approached. The flies rose in a huge cloud. The noise increased. They hovered momentarily above their prey, then sank back down again. They were in the air long enough for Anna to see the silver of the gorilla's back. And to see what the poachers had done to him.

'Oh,' she said. She steadied herself against a tree, feeling her legs about to buckle under her. Beside her, James heaved with nausea.

Another silverback lay a few metres away. He lay

on his side, his arms in front of him, his hands clasped together, his legs drawn up. He looked as though he slept. Except he lay in a pool of blood, his life inexorably drained away through the bullet holes in his great chest. As Anna and James approached him they noticed his arms and legs were bound. He was trussed, ready to be carried down the mountain. A long, newly cut, wooden pole lay on the ground beside him, in readiness.

A third gorilla sat with his back against a tree.

This one, in a way, was the worst. He too was tied at the hands and feet. But he seemed unharmed. No bullet wounds scarred him, no blood seeped from him. He just sat, as he would have done in life. Resting.

Anna fancied she saw his chest rise and fall.

'James, that one's still alive.' She walked towards him. Shock made her feel strangely disembodied, as though her legs did not belong to her.

'Be careful,' James warned.

But he wasn't alive. It had been a trick of the light perhaps, that had made him seem to move. The shadow of a branch, nudged by a bird, which had passed across his chest and made him seem to breathe. Or perhaps just wishing it to happen had lent reality to illusion.

He was dead. Eyes wide open, he stared at James and Anna as they came close to him. They looked into his eyes. His final, dying bewilderment and fear were distilled in them.

They stood in silence for long minutes. The flies whirred and hummed.

'Bush meat,' Anna said, softly. 'That's what they call it. They're taking them down to sell for meat.'

'Yes,' James replied. He sighed heavily. 'What did we say yesterday about there still being gorillas left alive?'

Anna turned to look at him.

'I sometimes wonder whether there'll be anything left alive in Rwanda. They kill each other, they kill the animals and the birds, they kill everything.' Her face was stricken.

'They kill anyone from a different tribe, just because they're not the same as them. It's always gone on. That's how things are. Just as they see no difference between animals. Killing a cow or a pig or a gorilla, it's all the same to them. It's all just food. It'll never end.'

'Come on, let's get away from here. I feel sick.'

They turned to move on. A movement in the trees on the far side of the clearing caught their eye.

'Shhh,' Anna whispered. 'There's somebody there.'

They inched silently back, away from the bloodied corpses of the gorillas, and crouched down behind some giant ferns.

Slowly, men began to emerge from the forest into the clearing.

'Oh no,' James whispered.

One by one the poachers returned. A big, shaven-headed man clad in ragged shorts and a sweatshirt with NEW YORK NEW YORK printed on it came first. A smaller man with an army coat next. And more men followed, similarly clad in a strange assortment of clothing. Sweating from the exertions of the climb, they slumped down on the ground, their weapons beside them.

Anna drew in her breath sharply at the sight of the weapons. A huge elephant gun lay beside one man, an automatic rifle beside another, and a collection of machetes and bows and arrows was distributed between the rest. The tools of their hideous trade.

One of the men produced a water bottle and passed it round. They all drank thirstily. One crossed to the fire, threw some more wood on it, then removed the blackened meat from the spit and began to tear at it with his teeth. Anna and James noticed his teeth were filed to sharp points. They shuddered involuntarily.

More men arrived.

The NEW YORK sweatshirt signalled the new arrivals to follow him. They crossed the clearing, making their way towards the dead gorillas.

James and Anna shrank farther back into the undergrowth.

A series of sharp orders delivered in Kinyarwanda followed. Four of the men strode over to the gorilla who lay on his side and began to thread the long wooden pole through the ropes binding his hands and feet. Groaning with the gorilla's great weight they hoisted the pole up on to their shoulders and readied themselves to carry him away.

More men turned their attention to the one sitting at the foot of the tree. Where James and Anna had almost wept to see a great creature reduced by senseless death to a tragic spectacle, these men seemed to find the gorilla funny. They gestured at him and laughed raucously, slapping their knees with mirth.

One bent his legs and began to lope around, arms swinging, thumping his chest POK POK POK and the others joined in with their voices WUH WUH WUH. They danced up to him, cavorting in front of him, mocking him in death as they would never had dared in life.

NEW YORK joined in the fun. He swaggered across to the seated figure, removed his baseball cap and sunglasses and placed them on the gorilla's head. Then he stepped back, regarded his handiwork and hooted with laughter. The cavorting and laughter of the others increased.

James grasped Anna's hand. They felt sick at the spectacle they were being forced to witness.

But the joke was soon played out. Foolish men lose interest quickly. And anyway there was a job to be done. The porters weren't being paid to fool about. NEW YORK signalled the laughter to stop and walked over to retrieve his cap and glasses. Then he stepped to the side of the gorilla, placed his foot against its shoulder and pushed. The gorilla slowly tipped to one side and fell over. A man slotted a pole through his ropes. Three more men joined him and they hoisted the gorilla up. By morning both gorillas would be down in the village markets, dismembered, butchered into convenient slabs of meat ready for the cooking pots and spits.

The porters began to move away. The limp bodies of the gorillas swung gently on the poles. Suspended by the hands and feet, heads lolling back, they looked as though they were traversing branches, creeping along, seeking food perhaps, a cruel parody of what they might have done in life. And as the grim procession crossed the clearing the poachers joked and laughed and nodded their heads and spat and gestured up the mountainside. Their meaning was clear. 'Don't be long coming back,' they were saying. 'There'll be plenty more for you to carry soon.'

Soon the porters had vanished into the forest leaving only the poachers behind. Excited by their mocking game some of them pranced and capered around for a while. Then they slumped to the ground laughing. The one wearing the army greatcoat produced a bottle of whiskey from one of its huge pockets and drank from it. Another snatched it from him, drank deeply and passed it on.

James and Anna watched silently from their hiding place.

They emptied the first bottle and another was produced. Soon the poachers' speech was slurred, their movements erratic, and their heads began to roll on to their chests. Eventually drunken snores and insensible grunts replaced their speech and laughter.

'OK,' said Anna when the moment appeared to be right. 'Let's go.'

Silently they crept away through the bush, skirted round the poachers and made their way back to the last tree James had marked.

'What now?' James asked. 'Go on, or back?'

'On,' said Anna. 'You saw what their intentions were.'

'Yes, but I don't see what we can do about that.'

'They've drunk themselves into a stupor. They'll be out cold till morning. That gives us some time at least.'

'Time to do what exactly?'

'Warn him they're coming. And before you ask me how, I don't know. But you saw what they did to those poor creatures. If we go away and do nothing it will be on our consciences for the rest of our lives.'

'Hmm,' James replied. 'And if we get involved with that gang back there, the rest of our lives may not be all that long.'

Anna smiled. 'Are you coming or not, then?'

'Of course I am.'

Sixteen

For the first few seconds Anna was unable to grasp what had happened.

She felt as though she had been delivered a great blow, viciously *slammed* by some force which had stunned her and driven all the breath from her body. She lay gasping for air.

Her mind reeled.

Suddenly she was not walking through the forest any more. Where she was now it was dark and wet and cool. She couldn't see anything. And there was a funny taste in her mouth.

Am I unconscious? her brain asked her. *Or dead? Is this what it's like to be dead?*

Then her eyes began to adjust. It wasn't completely dark.

She was lying, face down, on damp earth.

They had fallen!

'JAMES!' she shouted.

'I'm . . . here,' James gasped. She felt him touch her shoulder. 'Right behind you.'

Anna rolled over, spitting the wet earth out of her mouth.

The light, she noticed, was coming from high above, from the jagged hole they had torn in the matting of leaves and branches as they had plunged through it.

James was lying on his back, propped up by his rucksack. His chest rose and fell rapidly as he fought for breath too. She shuffled up to him and lay beside him.

'Are you all right?'

'Just winded, I think. We fell with quite a crash. Just give me a second, will you.' He struggled to get his arms out of the straps of his rucksack. 'And help me out of this thing, can you?'

She dragged the rucksack from underneath him and then they held each others' hands tightly for reassurance while their tortured breathing slowed.

Anna ran her tongue over her top lip and tasted blood.

'I've split my lip,' she said. She rolled over, then pushed herself up on to her hands and knees. She winced and rubbed her spine with the back of her hand. 'And hurt my back. Banged it on something.'

'Oh no,' James said. 'Badly?'

Anna slowly straightened up, groaning a little.

'Just bruised,' she announced. 'I think.'

'Right,' James said. 'I'm getting my breath back.' He sat up.

They looked around.

They were silent for a long time as they assimilated where they were.

The pit had been made with a large animal in mind. Buffalo at least, perhaps even elephant. It was about four metres long and at least three wide. Rows of stakes reared wickedly upwards from the floor of the pit, their ends sharpened to vicious points.

'No one can say we don't lead charmed lives,' observed James grimly.

Anna sat down again, her back against the cold earth of the pit wall.

They looked upwards at the patch of light.

'How high, do you think?' she asked.

'Five metres, I would guess.'

A long silence.

Five metres.

'Don't worry,' said James. 'The main thing is we're not badly hurt. Just give me a minute or two to recover and then I'll start figuring out how we're going to get out of here.'

He pulled the rucksack across and took out the water bottle.

'Here, bathe your lip.'

'Thanks. I've got a mouth full of soil too.' Anna took a swig of water, rinsed her mouth, turned her head and spat the water out. From the corner of her eye she thought she saw something move in the dim, far corner of the pit.

She stared hard into the gloom.

The shadows stirred, shifted.

Uncoiled.

'James,' she gasped, 'there's a snake or something over there.'

She started to scramble to her feet.

James grabbed her hand.

'Whoa. Go steady. I can't see anything. And if there is anything there it will be more afraid of you than you are of it.'

Anna took a deep breath and swallowed hard.

'Hmm,' she said, unconvinced. 'Maybe. Let's get out of here anyway.' She turned her attention to the walls. She dug her hands into the soil. It oozed between her fingers.

'Well,' she said, 'it's obvious we can't climb out. The soil's too wet. You can't get a purchase.'

James pondered the sides of the pit, allowing his eyes to rise slowly up the walls, searching for anything which might give some help. There was nothing. He turned and started to scan the other walls. All were equally unassailable. His heart sank.

Anna followed his eyes and drew the same conclusions. Then she noticed, near the tops of the walls, tangles of roots poking through, sent down by saplings growing at the pit's edges. They extended about a metre down into the topsoil.

'How tall are you, James?'

'Why? What are you thinking?'

Anna pointed up at the roots. 'If I stood on your shoulders, would I reach those roots?'

'Hmm. Worth a try.'

With much grunting they manoeuvred themselves until Anna was sitting on his shoulders. Then James backed them into the corner of the pit.

'Right,' he said. 'If you brace yourself against the walls you should be able to get your feet up on to my shoulders.'

Slowly she inched first one foot up, then the other. James grasped her ankles to hold her steady, then turned so they faced the walls again.

Anna reached up and scrabbled at the soil. Her hands were still half a metre away from the nearest of the roots.

'Any luck?' James's voice was strained with the effort of holding her.

'No, it's no good. Let me down.'

'So much for that brilliant idea,' Anna observed despondently when she was down again.

'How far away were you?'

'Too far.'

'Next try then,' said James, dragging the rucksack into the corner. 'We can gain some height by standing on this. It's packed so tightly, it's steady enough to use as a step.'

This time her searching fingers were short of salvation by about a quarter of a metre.

'How about this time?' James asked.

'It's no good. I still can't reach. I'll have to come down again.'

'Stay there,' James instructed. 'Steady yourself against the walls. I'm going to try lifting you.'

His hands moved from her ankles and grasped her boots.

'Ready?' he asked.

'Yes.'

James grunted as he began to push her up. She rose, desperately slowly. She strained her arms upwards, staring at the roots, mentally willing the gap between them and her fingers to close.

And then, slowly, she began to descend again. Until her feet were once more on James's shoulders.

'I couldn't do it,' he gasped. 'I just didn't have the strength to do it. We're finished. Come down again.'

'Don't say that,' Anna said. 'We can't just give up like that. We *can't*. Try once more.'

'It's no good. I'm not strong enough.'

'You are. You are! *Try once more*!'

'All right! Once more.'

And, with painful slowness, she felt herself begin to move upwards again. Her hands slid against the wet earth. Every muscle of her body and her brain was concentrated in her fingers, stretching them to the limits, reaching, reaching to the life-saving roots.

And, once again, stopped short.

'A little more,' she gasped. 'Just a little more.'

'I . . . can't . . . I . . . just . . . can't,' James whispered, his voice harsh. 'I've no more to give. No . . . more. I . . . can't . . . do it.'

His strength failed and she began to slip slowly back down again.

They were finished.

Then, so suddenly that there was no time to realize what was happening, there was a crashing of foliage, the heavy thump of feet and a blinding increase in light as the matting of the pit's roof was ripped away.

Anna had a fleeting, unreal impression of a dark figure looming above her and a waft of sweet, fruit-laden breath. Then a great, black arm reached down, a powerful, warm-leather hand gripped her arm, whisked her out into the sunlight and sat her down on the edge of the pit.

'Oh!' she gasped, momentarily baffled.

The gorilla moved away immediately, grunting excitedly. He lurched over to a tree, lashed out at the foliage as though in a temper, then turned and looked at Anna.

Anna stared back. He angled his head to one side and stared quizzically at her. The black leather face held no threat, the liquid brown eyes were inquisitive.

'ANNA!' James's voice sounded far away, muffled.

The gorilla turned his head at the sound. He grunted a reply.

Wuh-wuh. Wuh-wuh.

Anna scrambled to her feet.

'It's all right,' she shouted. 'I'm all right.'

'What's happening?'

Anna kneeled at the pit's edge and looked down.

'It's him. He heard us! He knew we were in trouble. He came to us.'

James stared up in incredulity from the depths of the pit.

The gorilla briefly glanced down, then began to shuffle away.

Anna's eyes followed him.

He remembered what to do. The lessons she had taught him in those first years when they had roamed the forest, finding the traps, the game they had together. Finding the wire snares on the ground, the nooses hidden in the branches, seeking out the pits, scenting the poisoned food.

Learning all the time, from her, what to do. Springing the traps. Releasing the trapped.

The memories remained. He knew what to do. He cast his eyes around, selected the tree he needed and loped across to it. He leaned forward, put his shoulder against the trunk and encircled it with his arm. He paused briefly, summoning all his strength. Then he opened his mouth and gave a great roar as he straightened up, putting all his immense weight and power behind one upward surge.

The tree succumbed immediately. There was a brief sucking of wet soil and it was ripped out of the ground. Its slender roots rose up into the air, whipping white and snake-like, scattering earth as they came.

He grunted with satisfaction, dropped the tree and began to drag it across the ground.

Anna gasped at the power of the movement. The tree he had pulled up was about ten metres tall, its trunk as thick as a man's leg.

'What's he doing?' James called. 'Has he gone?'

'No. Just wait a second. He's doing something. I'm not sure what he's doing it for, but he seems to know.'

And then she watched in amazement as this great, dark creature, gasping now with the effort of his strange, self-imposed task, hauled the tree across to the pit and slid it at an angle down into it. He stared briefly over the edge, grunted a couple of times softly, then moved away again.

Seconds later James appeared at the rim. Anna grasped his hands and helped him out.

'Miraculous,' James gasped. 'I can barely believe it.'

The gorilla grunted once, surveyed them for a second or two, then turned and began to walk away.

Anna watched him.

'That proves it,' she said. 'That was learned behaviour. He knew exactly what to do. He came because he heard our distress. He came to rescue us. He wouldn't know how to do that unless he'd been taught.'

Anna's eyes followed the creature's back as he began to melt away into the trees.

'It's him. There's no doubt. It's Doctor Hudson's "Shadow".'

It seemed to her as though he faltered slightly in his step. The tiniest of hesitations. As if he had heard her. As if he understood.

She called softly to him.

'Shadow? Shadow?'

He did not turn round at first, though Anna, waiting, knew he would.

He paused, still as a gravestone, for a long time.

Anna began to walk towards him.

He turned and watched her as she approached.

'Shadow?' Anna repeated softly as she came near. 'Shadow?'

He grunted.

Wuh-wuh-wuh.

Finally she stopped in front of him. She reached out her hand. He watched the movement, but did not respond. She kept her hand stretched out to him. But he would not take it, would not reach out to her.

'All right, Shadow,' Anna whispered eventually, dropping her hand. 'It doesn't matter.'

He grunted at the sound of his name. Puzzlement passed across his eyes. He turned his great head and stared behind him, up the mountain, then back at Anna. He grunted again as his eyes came to rest once more upon the girl.

'Oh yes,' said Anna. 'We know who you are.'

She raised her hand again and held it out to him, palm upwards, inviting him to put his hand in hers.

'Shadow?' she said softly.

And slowly, very slowly, a great black arm extended towards her. His long fingers gently touched her hand.

The touch lasted no time at all. The tiniest of contacts, fingers brushing a palm. Over as soon as it began.

Then Shadow rose and began to move away.

After a few paces he stopped and sat down.

Anna and James became aware now of faint rustlings in the trees. Shadow grunted softly to the sounds, reassuringly.

Very slowly the rest of the group began to assemble. They did not emerge from the trees, but a youngster chattered an inquiry, and an older female responded.

Shadow reached out to some nearby foliage, tore off a branch and began to eat. This action obviously signalled normality, for Anna and James felt the atmosphere change as the others relaxed. An infant came out and regarded them with interest and an old, greying female emerged and sat beside a tree close to Shadow.

A young female carrying a baby on her back cautiously approached Shadow and sat near him. The baby was coughing gently. A young male strutted out and sat beside her. He stared straight at Anna and James suspiciously.

But there was no aggression at all.

Shadow had signalled acceptance.

Anna looked round, from one gorilla to another. She stared hard at the trees at the ones too shy to emerge.

'You see, we have to do something,' she whispered eventually to James. 'Look at them, poor things. For all we know they're the last left.'

'Yes.'

She turned and looked back down the mountain,

to where the poachers lay in their drunken sleep. 'And now's the time to do it,' she said.

She beckoned to Shadow.

'Come,' she said.

At first he did not move to follow her. He watched her carefully, head on one side, then the other, studying her.

She beckoned again.

'Come, Shadow. Come with me.'

And he remembered once more the games they had played. The days when they had walked the forest together, the things she had shown him and the rewards she had given. And in his mind, lingering from infancy, there remained the pleasure of human company, the trust that had been there before his mind had been poisoned by a lifetime of conflict with man.

Shadow rose and began to follow Anna. The black-backs fell in behind.

'What are you going to do?' James asked.

'I'll explain as we go,' Anna replied.

Seventeen

They made a strange picture as they descended the mountain. The boy and girl close together leading the way, the great silverback creeping quietly along a few metres behind, soft feet shuffling, knuckles punching softly into the ground, the blackbacks uncertainly scuttling in and out of view.

James shook his head in disbelief. Shadow followed them as though he trusted them totally. Sometimes he stopped and turned to the blackbacks, reassuring them. Further back, the trees moved and foliage rustled as the rest of the group kept them in sight but remained at a safe distance.

'He knew his name,' James remarked. 'That's what gave him the confidence in you.'

'I know. I saw the recognition in his eyes. He remembers who he is. I think he probably remembers Doctor Hudson too. Or at least not her exactly, but the time with her. He remembers her lessons, that's for sure. The fact that we're alive and walking down here is proof of that.'

The gorillas became uneasy as they approached the poachers' camp. The smell of death and blood was in the air. The blackbacks lashed out at foliage in agitation as they began to realize what lay ahead. Shadow growled and silenced them.

But the fear the men engendered was very great.

The all-consuming fear of the gun. Even in Shadow. Even he began to hang back and, eventually, he stopped. The blackbacks stopped with him. They yawned nervously, crept into dense foliage and silently sat down.

Anna carried on and James had no choice but to follow. Soon they were back to where the mutilated gorilla carcass lay on the ground. Back to the place where they had hidden before.

Peering carefully through the foliage they surveyed the poachers. Things were just as they had left them. Snoring, drunken bodies littered the ground. The men's weapons lay at their sides. The automatic rifle was beside NEW YORK, its bullet clip in place. The long elephant gun lay beside Army Coat. Those two were the most dangerous.

'OK,' Anna whispered. 'You take NEW YORK. I'll take Army Coat.'

Silently they emerged into the clearing and, hearts thumping in their chests, crept across towards the sleeping men. The stench of whiskey hung on the air. Anna felt nausea at the sweetness of it as it mingled with fire and sweat and the horror-filled odour of cooked meat.

The men lay on their backs with their mouths wide open. In truth they were so stupefied that stealth was hardly necessary. Neither NEW YORK nor Army Coat stirred as James and Anna removed their weapons, crept back beyond their hiding place and concealed the guns under a dense carpet of moss at the foot of a *Hagenia*.

They returned to the edge of the clearing and planned the next sortie.

142

'The machete beside Blue Shorts for you,' James suggested. 'Bow and arrows beside Frilly Shirt for me. OK?'

'OK,' Anna whispered.

A minute later they were hiding more weapons in the moss.

'Like taking candy off babies,' Anna observed happily. She looked back up the slope and saw Shadow watching her from beside a tree.

'Once more and we've cleaned them out,' James added. 'Another couple of bows and arrows and that's it, I think.'

They returned to their task.

'You take Sports Jacket,' Anna said. 'I'll deal with the Fat One.'

Perhaps overconfidence made them careless. As Anna bent to pick up the bow she lost her balance slightly and staggered, nudging the sleeping man with her foot. He snorted loudly, then rolled over towards her and opened his eyes. There was a second of drunken incomprehension, then realization dawned. He shot out his hand and grabbed Anna by the wrist, pulling her down to the ground beside him. At the same time he bellowed a warning.

The others began to stir.

Anna screamed.

James spun round and ran across to her. He took hold of her by her other arm and tried to wrest her from the poacher's grasp. There was a moment's fierce struggle then James caught a whiff of whiskey-laden breath. Almost at the same instant he was grasped round the waist by powerful arms, lifted off his feet and dragged away from Anna. He kicked and struggled, but his captor was immensely strong and carried him effortlessly across the clearing. Behind him he heard Anna shout in pain as she was wrenched to her feet.

The NEW YORK shirt loomed up in front of him.

James's captor held him very still while NEW YORK surveyed the situation. He looked blearily around the clearing with incredulity in his eyes, first at Anna, then at James, then at the ground where their weapons should have been.

As comprehension grew so did his rage. He snarled in fury, stepped towards James and drew back his arm readying to strike him.

James prepared himself for the blow.

But before it could be delivered the man's eyes flicked upwards, looking past James towards the trees. Pure terror passed across his eyes. He turned and fled.

The poacher holding James was, for a second, confused. But a second was all he had. Briefly they heard the thump of soft feet. Immediately the man released his grip. James fell to the ground and rolled away, out of danger.

He came to a stop and watched fascinated. The poacher, as though weightless, was whisked off his feet by one of the blackbacks and hurled against a tree. The action was so effortless as to be contemptuous. There was a thud. The man crumpled as he hit the tree's trunk. He fell at its base as though made of rag and lay very still.

James shuddered. Then turned his attention to helping Anna.

His help was not needed.

Another blackback had hold of Anna's tormentor and had sunk his great teeth into the man's shoulder. He was worrying him, shaking him like a terrier with a rat. The man was thrown this way and that, screaming with pain and terror. The blackback picked him up and threw him across the clearing. He landed with a heavy thump on the ground. He rolled to his feet and ran away into the trees.

Then, within seconds, the clearing emptied as the terrified poachers fled. Helpless now, their courage buried with their weapons, they pounded away down the mountainside with the gorillas in hot pursuit.

James and Anna were left alone.

Anna sat down on the ground. James joined her. They were both trembling. They listened to the crashings and bellowings and frantic shouts of the chase.

'You all right?' Anna asked eventually, as her breathing steadied.

'Yes. I think so.'

A drawn-out scream floated up to them from the forest below.

Anna shivered briefly. But the picture of what they had found in this place was too fresh, too horrible, for her to feel any sympathy, or wish any mercy, for the fleeing men.

'We did the right thing, didn't we?' she asked.

'Of course we did,' James replied. He smiled with satisfaction.

The slaughtered were being avenged.

The wheel had turned.

Eighteen

'What time is it?'

James looked at his watch.

'Coming up to 5.30. We're all right. We've a bit of time left yet before dark.'

They were following the markers back down through the forest to the cabin.

'I wonder if any of the poachers escaped?' She looked around anxiously.

James shook his head. 'I doubt it. They'd need to be fast. I can't believe the speed those blackbacks took off after them. Anyway, our guard is still with us.'

Shadow and the blackbacks had kept pace with them, but a few metres to each side of them in the forest. Now and then their presence was heard as they pushed aside a tree, or glimpsed, dark shapes sliding from shafts of low, reddening sun into shade.

'Yes, I keep catching sight of them,' Anna said. 'Do you really think that's what they're doing?'

'I don't know. It's a nice idea. Perhaps they're just curious. Watching what we're doing. I'd like to think they're seeing us back safely.'

'I'm sure Shadow is doing that. He connects us with Doctor Hudson's cabin now, perhaps. His cabin too really. In a way he was brought up there. It's part of his life as well. Doctor Hudson said he kept coming back to see her. Perhaps he's been coming back all his life. Even when she'd gone.'

'Perhaps. I'll certainly be glad to get back there. Even with the gorillas' protection I don't fancy spending the night in the open forest. Let's concentrate on getting there.'

They continued down the mountain, from marker to marker. Now and then a glint of curious eyes from the shadows of a bush betrayed their escorts' position.

Dusk was falling as they descended the last 30 metres to the cabin.

'Just a minute,' Anna said. She grasped James by the arm and halted him.

'What?'

'Smoke. I saw smoke. Through the trees.'

Shadow saw them stop and moved closer, curious.

They moved slowly and cautiously on down until, through a gap in the trees, they could make out the cabin's roof.

Smoke was rising from the stove's chimney.

They continued a little farther until they could see the clearing. Their hearts sank. A couple of uniformed soldiers lay sprawled outside the front door.

Then, quite clearly, through the door, the figure of Dominic Seregera emerged. The soldiers were Hutu.

'Dominic,' Anna shouted. 'We're here.'

They started to hurry down to greet him.

Dominic stepped out into the clearing and looked up the mountain slope. He waved and called out to James and Anna.

'How did you find us?' Anna shouted.

Dominic laughed. 'A bull elephant would have left less of a trail,' he shouted back. Then he started to walk up to meet them. One of his Hutu guards rose to his feet and followed.

And as they looked up the slope at the descending figures, to their right, moving through the trees they both saw, indistinct but threatening, a large, dark shadow, moving towards them. Dominic drew his breath in sharply and signalled to the guard.

'Buffalo,' he snapped. 'Or something. There, to the right of them.'

The guard slipped his automatic rifle off his shoulder, flicked off the safety catch, took brief aim and released a hail of bullets.

The howl of pain and shock halted them in mid-step and froze their hearts.

'No-o-o-o-o!' Anna screamed.

There was a second's stunned silence. Then the blackbacks erupted into frightened yelps and started back up the mountain.

Another cry came from Shadow. A cry of mingled pain and anger and bewilderment.

'He's been hit!' Anna shouted. 'James! Shadow's been hit.'

She turned and started to run towards him.

James grabbed her and held her. 'Wait.'

Another cry, long, drawn out.

And then they heard him begin to pound away, following the blackbacks up the mountain.

Anna struggled free from James and ran through the trees to where Shadow had been.

'Oh,' she gasped.

A pool of blood had accumulated on the ground where he had stood, paralysed briefly by the suddenness of shock. Then spots of blood led away, upwards, betraying his flight.

James joined Anna, followed by Dominic and the guard.

Anna turned on them, her face contorted with fury and sadness.

'Do you know,' she screamed at them, 'what you have done?'

She turned and ran after Shadow.

He returned, in his dying minutes, to the place always destined for his return. Brought back by memory long hidden, now restored. Connected to this place by trust and loss, his feet could have carried him nowhere else.

Things had, of course, changed. Time had passed.

He had not been here since it had happened. And that was a lifetime ago.

But the changes were slight. The lifetime of an animal or a human is very brief. The forest, old beyond counting, has watched implacably as creatures, species, have come and gone. Like a travelling theatre show a new troupe of players appears now and then and performs its play. But, no matter how great or trivial, tragic or happy the events, hardly ever, when the curtain falls, is there a significant mark left behind.

The forest, the earth, just carries on. The rocks remain.

So things were much the same. Some trees were bigger perhaps, some saplings had appeared here, some ancient trees had succumbed to time and fallen there. But the place was, in its essence, as he remembered it.

The great tree trunk which had fallen on her had rotted with time. It was still there, still recognizable in shape, but decay and voracious termites had reduced it to a shell, a frail parody of what it once had been. It looked insubstantial now, flimsy, harmless.

He grunted as his gaze scanned the clearing and came to rest on the trunk. He put his head to one side and regarded it. The movement made him dizzy and he staggered with weakness. He put his uninjured hand up to his shoulder and held the pain that was there. It was wet with his blood.

He was afraid. But it was remembered fear. He looked upwards, opened his mouth, drew back his lips over his fangs and snarled up into the forest canopy, hearing again in memory the groaning noise as the trunk, delicately, artfully balanced, loosened and began its murderous fall.

He shuffled over to the trunk and stood looking at it. The fear it evoked, the nerves in the pit of the stomach, caused him to grunt rhythmically.

Wuh-wuh-wuh-wuh-wuh.

A snake slithered out from its dark lair in the tree's decomposed centre and hissed angrily at him. He lurched back, startled, then snarling with shock and revulsion, lashed out at it with his fist. An instinctive killing-blow of tremendous force.

The snake was too quick for him. Instantly it retracted and vanished, faster than vision, back into its hiding place. His fist plunged into the pulpy rottenness of the log, shivering it along its length, sending flakes of the fibrous remains of the once iron-hard wood showering into the air. He roared out as his wounds poured pain into his body. He breathed deeply until the pain subsided.

Something white caught his eye among the dusty remains of the log.

He put his head to one side and pondered it, examined it curiously.

He cried out once. A cry of grief, of loss remembered.

OOOOOM-AAAAAGH!

And then an immense weariness took hold of him. He dragged himself away from the log and slumped down at the base of a tree.

It was dark. It was time to sleep.

Moonlight is sad light.

Anna stood close to Shadow. He leaned against a tree, his great form crumpled, diminished by death. The moon had sucked the colour out of his black pelt, silvered him. Cruelly made a ghost of him. But it could not dull the scarlet of his blood.

'Look,' Anna said sadly. 'He's tried to pull branches around himself. Tried to make a nest.'

'That's the beauty of being an animal perhaps.' James sighed heavily. 'You don't understand death. Perhaps he just thought he was going to sleep.'

No one believed him.

'I'm sorry,' Dominic said.

'It wasn't your fault,' Anna replied. She turned away, tears in her eyes. 'You did what seemed right. It was a mistake. An understandable mistake. That's all.'

'Perhaps the mistake was ours,' James said. He gazed, anguished, at Shadow. 'Doctor Hudson tried to teach him that trusting humans was dangerous. He trusted us. And this is the result.'

'No,' Anna said gently. She put her hand on his arm, understanding his pain. 'You mustn't think that. He came to us first, remember? Perhaps trust was what he was seeking, what he needed from us. And he found it. We must be thankful for that.'

'It's all so senseless. So much violence everywhere. So much death. Look at him. He sums it all up. Nearly the last of his kind. What's it all about?'

'Nothing. It's not about anything. It's just the way things are. Things happen, that's all.' She stepped up to Shadow and gently touched his head. 'Poor thing. He saved our lives. I only wish we could have saved his.'

She noticed something white glinting in the moonlight on the other side of the clearing. She crossed and knelt down. She scraped away the fibrous shreds of the dead wood.

'James,' she called, softly. 'Come here.'

She scraped more. The bones of a human skeleton began to appear.

James knelt and joined her.

Gently they brushed away the rotten wood until most of the skeleton was revealed. A few remnants of clothing still clung to it. Round its neck, tarnished, dulled with age, a silver pendant hung askew.

Anna reached down and gently unclasped it. It was small and delicate. She turned it over and rubbed the back.

It bore a simple inscription.

JAH

'Oh,' said Anna softly.

She turned and looked back across the clearing.

A cloud moved across the moon. The great gorilla's form grew black again, the ghost-silver was stripped away, the blood concealed. Restored by darkness, he became, briefly and from a distance, Shadow again.

'He came back,' she whispered. '*He came back to her.*'

They carried him down in the morning and buried him next to the others.

Then they collected their things and prepared to leave.

'Straight over the top and into Uganda,' Dominic ordered. 'We contacted the British Embassy by radio. Your parents are safe in Kenya and there will be Ugandan soldiers to meet you at the border. My guards will escort you all the way there.'

'Thank God they're safe. But what about you?' Anna asked. 'What will you do?'

'I have no choice in what I do. The Hutu are leaderless now my father is dead. I must stay and try to help.'

'Will it ever end?' James asked.

'No.' Dominic shook his head. 'Not until all the Tutsi are gone. Or all the Hutu.' He turned and strode away down the mountain. 'Goodbye. I wish you luck. You will soon be safe, I'm sure.'

James and Anna fell in with the guards and they began to make their way upwards.

'Just like on the mountain,' Anna observed. 'We won one round yesterday with the poachers. But they'll be back. They'll always be back. So it won't ever end here either.'

Nineteen

They approached the summit in late afternoon.

'All right, Anna?' James asked.

'Yes, I'm all right. The time on the mountain has made the altitude easier.'

A cold wind blew across the high, barren peak. It swirled a diaphanous, ghostly mist around them. A pale sun battled with the mist and now the mountain below them would be revealed, now obscured.

'Just a few more steps to safety.'

Anna turned and looked back down the mountainside.

'For us,' she said. 'Safety for us.'

She stopped.

'I think I'd like to sit here just for a minute,' she said. 'Before we go over the top.'

'That's fine.'

The guards walked on a little, then waited.

Through the pale mist, Rwanda stretched out before them. Poor, racked Rwanda. It seemed so quiet, so peaceful, so beautiful from up here. It was hard to believe, high above its silent green landscape, that lives were being torn apart, that horrors beyond imagination were taking place in its quiet villages.

'I suppose her father will be dead now,' Anna

mused. 'If he is, he would have died never knowing what happened to her.'

'Perhaps. If he is alive he'll be very old now. It would be nice if we could set his mind to rest. We'll contact Cambridge University as soon as we get settled in Uganda. The British Embassy will do it for us.'

'I hope he is. I'd like to meet him. Tell him about Shadow.'

'Yes.'

'And give him her locket.'

'Perhaps. We'll see. I think we should go now. We've still got to get down the other side, before dark if we can.'

'Just a minute more,' Anna whispered.

They sat in silence for a while.

'Why do people do it? Kill each other? Kill animals? Kill everything?'

James was silent. There was no reply to give. No reply expected.

Anna shivered. 'Come on,' she said. 'I'm getting cold.'

They stood, turned their backs on Rwanda and walked to the top of the mountain.

A small stone cairn, a monument built by hands which wished to leave a human presence on this most remote and desolate of mountains, marked the summit. From it, on the ground, three lines of stones formed arrows, pointing the way for travellers. The one pointing back to Rwanda had been kicked and scattered. They walked past the cairn, on to Ugandan soil. Briefly they stopped.

'Do you think we'll ever come back?' James asked.

Faintly, from below, Anna thought she heard a solitary gorilla cry out.

'Yes,' she whispered, answering the cry. 'We'll be back.'

Glossary

askari	guard
ikibooga	poacher's den
kanga	wrap-around garment
shambas	gardens

The Shark Callers

Sliding silently and with effortless strength along the silver highways of the sea, the sharks are waiting . . .

Andy and his family sail the seas off Papua New Guinea – until their boat is wrecked by a terrifying volcanic eruption.

Kaleku is also at sea – in his fragile canoe. Alone he must lure and kill a shark, to earn his place as a shark caller.

Two boys from two different worlds – but the ocean's deadliest killer awaits them both . . .

The Year of the
Leopard Song

Kimathi always knew he was marked out. But now the time has come. Now he must go up into the snows of Kilima Njaro, the roof of all Africa, to the Place of Song. The place of danger.

The word CHUI – leopard – written in blood is one of the first signs. It spoils the joy of Alan's return to the farm after a year at school in England.

Then his friend Kimathi disappears, and Alan knows he must climb the high slopes of Mount Kilimanjaro to find him. But terrifying danger awaits Alan – for he is following the leopard song . . .

Elephant Gold

Fifty years ago. And not a day without the memory.

For half a lifetime the poacher and the elephant have been enemies. Since the shattering day when the man massacred the young animal's herd – and paid in his own blood.

Now the poacher is about to wreak his revenge at last. To slaughter the mighty elephant that maimed him. As man and beast move towards one final, terrible encounter, only one person can prevent a tragedy. The young girl who loves the elephant more than her life . . .

Books by Eric Campbell
available from Macmillan

The prices shown below are correct at the time of going to press.
However, Macmillan Publishers reserve the right to show new retail
prices on covers which may differ from those previously advertised.

ERIC CAMPBELL
Gorilla Dawn   0 333 73841 1   £9.99
The Place of Lions   0 330 31977 9   £3.99
The Shark Callers   0 330 32999 5   £3.99
The Year of the Leopard Song   0 330 32408 X   £3.99
Elephant Gold   0 330 34728 4   £3.99

All Macmillan titles can be ordered at your local bookshop
or are available by post from:

Book Service by Post
PO Box 29, Douglas, Isle of Man IM99 1BQ

Credit cards accepted. For details:
Telephone: 01624 675137
Fax: 01624 670923
E-mail: bookshop@enterprise.net

Free postage and packing in the UK.
Overseas customers: add £1 per book (paperback)
and £3 per book (hardback).